I0540011

VIETNAM AMBUSH

SOLDIER IN THE BUSH

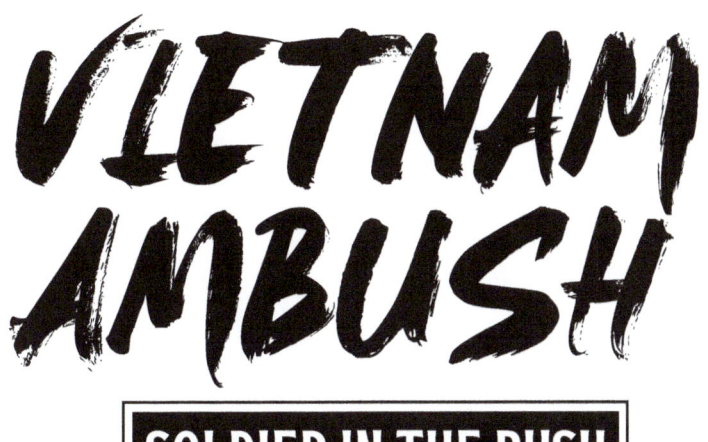

VIETNAM AMBUSH

SOLDIER IN THE BUSH

DANIEL SEIDENBERG JR.

Kravitz & Sons

INNOVATORS IN PUBLISHING, MARKETING AND ADVERTISING

Kravitz and Sons LLC
1301 Farmville Blvd, Suite 104
Greenville, NC 27834

© 2024 Daniel Seidenberg JR. All rights reserved.

No part of this book may be reproduced, stored in a retrieval system, or transmitted by any means without the written permission of the author.

Published by Kravitz and Sons LLC.
ISBN: 979-8-89639-026-8 (sc)
ISBN: 979-8-89639-025-1 (e)

Library of Congress Control Number: 2024925378

Because of the dynamic nature of the Internet, any web addresses or links contained in this book may have changed since publication and may no longer be valid. The views expressed in this work are solely those of the author and do not necessarily reflect the views of the publisher, and the publisher hereby disclaims any responsibility for them.

TABLE OF CONTENTS

This book is dedicated to my wife Anna, sons John and Christopher and to my dear friend, Reggie Kennedy as well as to all of the soldiers who served with D-5/12, 199th Light Infantry Brigade in the Vietnam War.

ACKNOWLEDGMENTS

I want to acknowledge and thank George Campion for his invaluable research at the National Archives in Washington D.C. without which this book would never have been possible.

My profoundly felt appreciation goes to Vietnam War Historian, Bernie Weisz for editing and giving me valuable advice for this second edition. Also to the late Robert Potter whose patient editing and help was crucial to finalizing the original manuscript for publication.

Special and warm thanks to all who read the manuscript and offered suggestions and other feedback; Ken McAlpine, Amy and Brendan Thorne, Tara Bushman, Josh Ellis, and Theodore Kennedy.

CHAPTER ONE

A WINTER SOLDIER

"These are the times that try men's souls. The summer soldier and the sunshine patriot will in this crisis shrink from the service of his country. But he who stands it now deserves the love and thanks of men and women."— Thomas Paine

The attrition rate for U.S. soldiers during 1968 and 1969 in Vietnam was the highest since our Civil War, when the casualties on both sides were Americans.

A combat patrol in World War Two and in Korea was a matter of hours. In Vietnam it was a matter of weeks.

The first casualty of war is the truth. If you were trying to get at it through the menacingly thick fog of war, the roar of a freight train speeding by, weariness experienced only by the nearly dead, then one begins to understand the difficulty remembering and writing it all down.

I was a combat infantryman in Vietnam. We were shooting dice for our souls. Our very spirits were on the line, if we survived.

No one could say what we were fighting for. The consensus was that our purpose was to simply survive it all. I knew that merely surviving would not be enough. I had to make sure that I survived with a clean conscience.

What good is living, if you wind up hating yourself? And I didn't want to be responsible for any crimes.

In a war fought entirely in cold blood, keeping a clean conscience and remaining alive was not easy.

I received my draft notice the winter of 1967. I had graduated high school that spring of 1966 and I was to report for induction the next summer. I didn't want to die. I was only 20, and life had barely begun. I saw no reason to kill the Vietnamese.

The Vietnamese had not attacked the USA, no firefights had taken place at Refugio beach, where I spent a lot of happy days surfing and sunning, safely away from the evening news and the myriad cares of small town southern California. I had barely heard of Vietnam.

When I pondered the draft notice, I felt that perhaps I ought to head for Canada. Before induction time, I actually went. I crossed the border with ease, north of Seattle, sat in a park in Vancouver, British Columbia, for hours.

I called an old friend that I knew in Tukwila, Washington. Ted had been in Korea with the army. We had met when I was in high school.

He'd been mowing his yard when I walked by on my way to the beach.

"Hey, why don't you help me mow this damn yard?"

"How about some gas money for the beach?" I answered with a laugh.

So I helped him finish the yard work and Ted gave me a couple of dollars. That was the start of a long and valuable friendship.

When Ted answered my phone call, he told me that I must make my own decisions but that he thought that if I did join the army, everything would be alright.

Finally I decided that being without a homeland and a family wasn't for me. Why was I any better than the thousands of other young men who had to go into the service?

How could I live with myself if I ran away from America? Hadn't my grandfather been an infantryman, wounded in World War One?

Hadn't my father flown many missions in the Army Air Corps during World War Two? I didn't want to believe that I was a coward.

Every third draftee was being inducted into the Marines. The Marines were combat troops and that was the last thing I ever wanted to do. I surely did not want to be a Marine, which was a lifelong career choice. If I had to go, I only wished to serve the minimum amount necessary, and then return to my real life.

I headed for the Seattle Army recruiting station to see what my alternatives were.

The recruiter was very personable and seemed to fully understand my dilemma. He said I could sign a two year contract with the regular Army and thereby avoid being drafted into the Marines. He also said that I would never see combat; "The war is over, the worst that could happen is that you wind up in the infantry guarding Korea."

That sounded good to my worried mind. I wanted to believe him, so I did. I signed and swore to protect our constitution from all enemies, foreign and domestic. I figured I could serve my country for two years and then carry on with a normal, civilian life afterwards. Six months later I was in combat in Vietnam.

Walking is the way of life in the infantry. They didn't call us "legs" for nothing. Walking while placing as little weight as possible with each step, although carrying 70 pounds of food, water and combat gear, at any moment your life could be blasted to shreds. Booby traps were everywhere, tied into bushes and trees, disguised as C ration cans, buried under trails.

My first day in the field, I almost sat on a fishing line that led to three Chinese manufactured hand grenades wired together in a bush about five feet away. If touched, they would have detonated.

We had taken a short break for lunch and the ground was wet everywhere so I decided to sit on my flack jacket to eat and rest. Just as I was about to put it down on the ground, I noticed the mono filament line. Following the line with my eyes, it led into a bush with the three grenades hanging in it like deadly Christmas tree ornaments. I stood up, put my flack jacket back on and told the sergeant what I saw. Then I found a spot with no booby traps to rest and eat.

That morning near sunrise, we had formed up for my first "Eagle Flight". After boarding the helicopters we ascended up and away with the chopper blades clapping and popping us a farewell. High in the sky, the land looked like a moonscape there were so many bomb craters.

After about half an hour we landed in a clearing and jumped out of the helicopters, grouped into marching order and began the combat patrol. The sound of a single bullet shot announced the presence of the war. We all hit the dirt.

I didn't know what would happen next and I expected to be shot at. Fear was hanging inside of my head, like bats in a cave. But nothing happened so we stayed down for what seemed like hours until word was passed that everything was OK. A fellow soldier close by said that Sergeant Hall had shot himself in the foot with his .45 caliber pistol.

A short while later, the captain said that Sergeant Hall would be medically evacuated and then he would be court-martialed for destroying government property: the bullet and his foot.

My thoughts screamed at me that this war was beyond anything I could comprehend. Why did he shoot himself? I asked, but no one answered.

When I was being trained at Fort Lewis, Washington, so many trainees had been going AWOL, [absent without leave] to Canada that the Army training cadres came up with a plan; they announced that none of us would be going to Vietnam because the war was over. On our last day at Fort Lewis, all of us did finally receive orders to report to Oakland Army Base for the flight to the Republic of Vietnam.

I asked the Captain; "Why are we were going to Vietnam, if the war is over?"

He answered: "To help the peasants."

One of the training cadres, a Vietnam combat veteran himself, added some sage advice; "Stay low to the ground, get into the shade and take a piss every chance you get."

Walter Cronkite had opined on his CBS newscast after the deadly battles of Tet 1968, the war was a stalemate. So I tried to believe what the cadre had said, but I knew it was wishful thinking at best.

On the flight to Vietnam, there were stops in Hawaii and the Philippines for refueling. It was a commercial flight, complete with perky stewardesses bubbling over with good humor and cheerful enthusiasm.

When we finally arrived at Tan Son Nhut airbase, the perpetually smiling stewardess said, "Welcome to Vietnam. I hope you all have a wonderful tour and I'll see you again in 365 days!"

Was this going to be some kind of tropical vacation?

Stepping out of the airplane, I felt the blast furnace air begin to bake me. It must have been nearly 100 degrees with almost as much humidity.

Wherever I looked, everyone was heavily armed. I had never seen so many weapons in my life. The air smelled of long dead animals, human sweat and excrement with diesel and jet fuel mixed in.

While descending the stairs leading from the airplane, I saw a huge sign hanging over the terminal entry that read; "WELCOME TO VIETNAM, LOVE IT OR LEAVE IT."

That night I slept at the Camp Alpha holdover barracks, a large shack with two rows of bunk beds. Camp Alpha was part of Tan Son Nhut airbase. No working doors or windows, just rows of cots on a plank floor with sandbagged plywood walls and a canvas ceiling.

Next morning I could not open my eyes. I thought to myself, "Maybe I've contracted some rare tropical disease already." So I headed for sick call using my fingers to pry and keep my eyes open enough to see.

When the medic looked at me, he laughed and said the swelling would go down soon. "You have to sleep with your head under the covers 'cause the mosquitoes will feast all night on your eyelids."

I spent a few days at Camp Alpha, carrying luggage for officers who were either arriving or departing. Then I was trucked a few miles over to the 90th Replacement Depot with a number of other new replacements. I spent another two days there before getting orders to report to the 199th Infantry Brigade located at Long Binh, not far from the replacement depot.

I felt lucky not to be going up north to the demilitarized zone that divided North from South Vietnam, or to the Central Highlands. I had heard that was where most of the heavy combat was occurring. Our area of operations, [AO], was mostly jungle, southwest of Saigon.

Arriving at my combat brigade near sunset, early in December, 1968; the sky was laden with massive grey clouds, a flimsy rain shining everything as it silently descended.

We replacements stood at attention as the rain became ever more robust. Studiously we listened while the colonel told us that the 199th Light Infantry Brigade had never left a trooper on the battlefield and never would.

I found little comfort in his remarks. I had just turned twenty-one a few weeks earlier…I was definitely not ready to die, regardless of where my remains might finally end up.

After the visit with the colonel, a sergeant showed me the way to my platoon's position on the perimeter. There, a fellow grunt, [we were called "grunts" because of the sound we made while walking and carrying our combat loads], introduced himself as Tex and welcomed me with a marijuana cigarette.

"No thanks, I don't feel like getting high right now."

He had a round rosy boyish face, pale blue eyes, short blond hair and a very solid build. His well muscled legs were carried by large, totally flat feet.

Tex laughed and puffed away then told me I would be taking the midnight to 0200 guard shift.

He also told me he had been in Vietnam for three months; was 18 years old and from Houston, Texas. He was in the Regular Army also. All of the other soldiers in our company were draftees. I asked him why he had joined and he said that he was looking for adventure, nothing more.

I told him I had joined to beat the draft. He couldn't stifle a belly laugh while trying to hold down his last puff of marijuana, coughing out a white smoke cloud along with a shower of saliva. Then he mentioned that our company was heading for the dreaded "Pineapple."

I looked around for a place to sleep. Everything in the small bunker was wet so I stacked some ammo boxes together, placed my poncho liner on top and lay down to rest on them.

Tex smoked away, laughing at everything I asked him. I was very tired and extremely scared but Tex's boyish laughter and cavalier nature seemed to calm me somewhat.

"Tex, how are we supposed to see anything in this darkness and rain?"

Tex laughed again, "You'll see a lot, don't worry, and besides, we have a starlight scope."

It seemed that as soon as I fell into a shallow slumber I was awakened by screeching noises coming from under the ammo boxes. The screeching grew ever louder. I sat up, looking around in the darkness and could barely make out small creatures, the size of kittens chasing and fighting each other. They were vying for room under my ammo boxes, apparently. There was no stopping them. The Vietnamese paddy rats fought, partied and copulated the entire night.

It was my turn for guard duty anyway, so I got up as Tex passed me the starlight scope and a wristwatch. He showed me who to wake up next and told me not to look through the starlight scope. He didn't tell me why.

Donning my helmet and flack jacket, I slept with my boots on; with my rifle I walked out of the tiny bunker and over to the sandbagged position near the concertina wire on our perimeter. It was still raining and I could just barely see my own hands.

I thought back to the morning that I was issued combat gear. Moving down the supply line at brigade headquarters, Long Binh main brigade base, getting a flack jacket, helmet, camouflaged helmet cover, jungle boots, gas mask, plastic canteens, pack and frame, ammo bandoliers, M16 rifle, rain poncho and liner, with the grumpy supply sergeant rushing me along.

I noticed that the M16 I was issued had some shrapnel holes in the heat guard that protected one's hands when the barrel got hot from firing numerous bullets. No doubt due to the misfortune of the previous owner. When I mentioned this defect, the sergeant told me that it still fired adequately.

Then I asked the supply sergeant for a bayonet saying, "You can't expect me to go into the jungle without one."

In training, at Fort Lewis, we had practiced with bayonets for weeks. Thrust, parry, thrust, parry, on and on, thrust and parry.

We had to yell out in reply to the cadre's call, "What is the spirit of the bayonet?"

"To KILL, KILL, KILL, KILL!" While thrusting and parrying.

The supply sergeant grumbled that he would not issue me a bayonet because, "You grunts just wind up throwing them at each other," so no bayonet.

When I mentioned this to Tex, he said that we could buy our own or write home to have knives mailed to us. I felt a bit more betrayed by the most well equipped army in the world.

I had to look through the starlight scope. I kept wondering why Tex had said not to. When I got the nerve to look, it appeared that I was seeing movement and human shaped silhouettes in its eerie, greenish, luminous eye piece. I felt like waking the others, but I resisted and kept looking for something more substantial.

Everything beyond the concertina wire seemed ominous and moving ever so slightly towards me, but maybe not. There were clumps of bushes and partially blown away tree stumps here and there within my view. Were the clumps perhaps disguising enemy soldiers out there? Maybe I simply needed practice looking through this scope?

Back and forth, my mind seemed to be playing a ping pong game. I had never felt this kind of fear.

I made it until my guard period was over, but just barely. When I passed the wrist watch and the scope to the next guard after gently waking him, I mentioned that I had seen strange things with it. He laughed, saying, "Thanks!" but nothing else.

I had seen the troops coming back from Vietnam at the Oakland Army Base the day I reported for deployment. They all looked very aged and tired, even though they were no older than I. None of them would look me in the eyes nor say anything to those of us on our way to the war. They all looked haggard, distant and emotionally numbed by their war experiences.

Now, after two hours of guard duty, I knew why fear was my closest and constant companion from that time on. It wasn't the fear of death, scary as that is. It was the fear of losing one or both legs. All of us feared this and the loss of our genitals the most.

I was asked more than once by fellow grunts, "If my legs are wasted, shoot me in the head."

At other times I was asked by someone to shoot them in the foot, so that they could get out of the field. Of course, I never could or ever would. But that made me think about it a lot.

There was also the fear of being a coward or of becoming a criminal that nagged me almost constantly. I didn't want to be responsible for killing anyone, much less a civilian. No one as yet had explained sufficiently why we were here or why we needed to kill people.

When my guard duty ended I went back to the ammo boxes and began thinking about my girlfriend back home. We had decided to break up after a last party in San Francisco the night before I was to report to Oakland army base for deployment to Vietnam.

I figured that I would possibly be dying in Vietnam and didn't want my girlfriend hurt. So we agreed to break up and to not write each other after crying for hours together, high on LSD. What a bummer that was.

Next day, leaving Oakland and flying above San Francisco, I kept hearing the song, "I Left My Heart in San Francisco" play over and over in my mind.

CHAPTER TWO

THE PINEAPPLE
War, fresh, daily.

"You can kill ten of my men for every one I kill of yours, but even at those odds, you will lose and I will win."—Ho Chi Minh

Operations continued in the western PINEAPPLE.

[Intelligence Summary, 199th Inf Bde {Sep} {Lt} INTSUM 54-69]

The sun was setting and we were still humping along, fording a small river. I was soaking wet when we arrived at our night ambush site. The mosquitoes were attacking and the sun had set. I was paired in a fighting position with Rob, a grunt that would be getting out of the field tomorrow. He was finishing his three hundred, sixty-five days and would be soon heading home.

The night was black. We couldn't see five feet in front of us. Some of the grunts were complaining about getting into an ambush site after dark when they could not see to lay out their fields of fire. Everyone was paired up and given fighting positions by the squad leaders. We were strung out in a long line of fighting positions, each about fifty feet apart.

Rob gave me the first watch as he wanted to rest right away. He also gave me some advice. "Do not fire your rifle, no matter what happens."

I could not understand why he would say this in the middle of a war. This area was called, after all, a "free fire zone" by the army commanders, meaning that everything that moved was considered to be the enemy. They also referred to it as "Indian Country" and as the "bush."

After a short time, I heard a swishing noise out in the blackness. It didn't go away, either. It sounded like people creeping up on us. Perhaps an entire battalion of enemy soldiers was low crawling our way. I was growing ever more scared as the sound caused my mind to engage in that ping pong game once again.

"Is that the enemy or my imagination?" Back and forth, back and forth, on and on the game went.

Then the sound of an explosion shattered the ping pong table. The table, balls and paddles went flying.

I felt panicky, scared and threatened as I reached for my rifle, flicked the safety off and fired off a burst of six rounds towards where the sounds were coming from.

Rob sat up and yelled at me, "DO NOT FIRE YOUR RIFLE!"

I told Rob that I thought we were being attacked.

"I don't want to hear about it," was his answer.

I sat my rifle back down and Rob covered his head again with his poncho liner and appeared to go back to sleep. Tex then scrambled into our position saying, "Tony reconned that noise with a hand grenade, why didn't you guys get word of it?"

"I don't know," Rob said, sitting back up and adding, "I don't need this shit." Then he covered his head once again while slipping back into a prone position.

I stayed wide awake for the rest of the night, waiting for the enemy to attack. I had a row of hand grenades ready for them, placed on the edge of my poncho liner upon which I was sitting. The swishing noise never let up at all the entire night.

When the sun came up enough to see around, I noticed a tiny creek about ten feet out in front of us that was causing the reeds and small bushes on its banks to sway back and forth producing the swishing noise. Now I understood why the other grunts had complained about getting into an ambush site after dark.

We made instant coffee and ate rations. I was very tired, nearly sleep walking.

The captain shouted, "Saddle up," we were moving out.

I was so tired that I couldn't see straight. I was still wet from boots to shirt, yet on we marched. The sun was high in the sky, scorching hot and had dried me out by the time we broke for chow around noon.

We boiled water in our helmets; they weren't called "steel pots" for nothing. We broke off small chunks of "C4" plastic explosive from the bars of it that we all carried and lit it to produce a small, yet very hot, blue-white fire to cook with.

The water would be boiling in less than ten minutes. The boiling water was then poured into a foil packet of freeze dried food that we called LRRPs, pronounced, "lerps", which was short for "long range reconnaissance patrol".

We ate without enthusiasm, preferring the light weight LRRPs over the heavier, olive drab canned, C-rations. Except for the canned fruit, that was highly prized, and was surplus from Korea or World War Two.

I opened a can of peaches to wash down my freeze dried beef and rice with. I was sitting next to a bush and noticed the small red ants living on it seemed to be very hostile. Many of them were actually reaching out for me when my arm came close. They had large mandibles with sharp pinchers. Tex told me if you get too close the whole colony would attack and all of them bite, drawing blood, holding onto your skin until you could strip down and pull them off one by one.

Even the ants here in Vietnam could be a kind of booby trap.

After about three hours on the march, the company was divided into numerous, four man "star teams." To my team, consisting of Tex,

Brownwood, Jim and myself, a gun crew was attached; Pappy and Dupree, a black teenager from Detroit, and their M-60 machine gun. So there were five of us manning my first day ambush. Pappy was from Puerto Rico. He was 26 years old, that's why he was called "Pappy". He spoke only Spanish.

On we "humped," [what we called walking], until Brownwood, the squad leader, told us to stop and set up our ambush. We were on a dyke which circumvented and enclosed a pineapple field. The pineapple field looked to be about the size of an average city block back in the states.

We moved into a small depression that was on the jungle side of the dyke system. The dyke ran like a raised trail, the length of our position. The machine gun crew was situated on the right flank and the rest of us were spread out for about twenty feet behind the machine gun and alongside of the trail.

Tex was lighting a cigarette when Pappy looked over his shoulder at us and put his finger to his lips, signaling us to be silent.

I saw a small man, dressed in black and carrying a rifle coming right towards us, walking on the dyke approaching our right flank. "He could toss a grenade at us now," I was thinking to myself.

Switching my M16 rifle off of "safety" with my thumb, I told myself to just watch what the others would do and learn from them for now. The man walked by our machine gun then looked directly at us. He quickly made a hard right turn and began running like an Olympic sprinter through the rows of pineapple bushes.

Brownwood told us to open fire at him. Tex stood up and began firing his rifle. Brownwood fired his M79 grenade launcher, and said: "I think I nicked the dink!"

The rest of us simply watched. I didn't want to make a mistake, being so new to this job.

The black pajama clad man finally made it to the other side of the pineapple field with Tex's bullets hitting in the mud around him. Making it to a large bush, he hit the ground looking like a major league ball player sliding into second base. Tex emptied a magazine and shoved another into his rifle. He kept firing into the bush where we last saw the man. Brownwood fired a couple more M79 grenades into that bush also.

Thinking what if he was the point man for a platoon or a company of Viet Cong soldiers, I began preparing myself for a counter attack, which thankfully never came.

Then I heard the sound of a helicopter chopping through the sky above us. It was the colonel; he was calling us on the radio, telling us what a hell of a good job we were doing and that he would be landing to see for himself.

Meanwhile Tex and Jim ran across the pineapple field, chasing the hapless man. They didn't find him but they did see blood on the bush and in the mud. A blood trail led off into the jungle.

Once the colonel was on the ground, he congratulated Tex, saying what a fine soldier he was. The colonel said he was very proud of us all.

Since most of us had not fired our weapons and Pappy had let the enemy soldier walk right by his fully loaded machine gun. I didn't agree with the accolades at all. It would be a long time or perhaps never, before I would understand this war.

The colonel's chopper departed as swiftly as it had arrived.

It was hot beyond belief; the sweat flowing down my forehead was burning my eyes. We all had towels draped around our necks to wipe our faces with.

Figuring the enemy certainly knew our position now, Brownwood received radioed permission to move our ambush site.

Sliding his pack on and after another swig from his canteen, he said, "Saddle up!"

My thoughts turned back to Trish, of all people. I had met her at the "Pit," a beach in Santa Barbara known for its occasionally surfable shore break. We decided to meet each other again, later at the Doors concert which was happening that night.

Trish and I sat on the beach, looking at the sparkling, undulating sea and into one another's eyes.

She told me about her life. We were about the same age, had both graduated from the same high school and had a lot of friends in common. We loved the beach; we soaked in the sun and sprawled in the sand until sunset.

I surfed in between our heartfelt conversations. Slashing hard turns and getting short tube rides. Trish read her book, "The Castle," by Franz Kafka.

We discussed everything it seemed, except the war. The war hung like a pall over everything. The war was an awful nightmare that reoccurred, day after day after day after day.

We purposely avoided that subject, but it was always in the back of our minds. The war was on television every night at dinner. The number of our soldiers killed that day had to be digested before dinner. It could not be escaped back home. And now I was right in the middle of it.

CHAPTER THREE

BOOBY TRAPPED

"War is fear cloaked in courage."—Gen. William C. Westmoreland

At 01614 hrs, a hunter-killer team, supported by helicopters from Fireball and Silver Spur, engaged one VC in a bunker. In a series of mishaps caused by rifle fire from the VC, one LOH received several hits and was forced into the canal and the Fireball helicopter went in to pick up the Silver Spur crewmen on the south bank. It received direct hits, rolled over on its back, and crashed. Shortly afterwards Fireball 113, with COL Jeffrey G. Smith, Deputy Commander, 199th LIB, as a passenger, arrived on station. In an attempt to recover the Silver Spur crew, Fireball 113 also received rounds and was forced down at FSB KATHY. Both crews were recovered and evacuated, one crewman was wounded in the foot and arm. Both members of the Cobra crew were killed. COL Smith and one door gunner from Fireball 113 were wounded.

[Intelligence Summary, 199th Inf Bde {Sep} {Lt} INTSUM 54-69]

Our radioman, [RTO], told us we were to move, quickly, to the site of a downed helicopter. We were all exhausted and wet. I couldn't understand how we could move any faster.

Brownwood said we ought to walk on the trail for speed. We did and after a short time there was an explosion directly behind me. I was walking "slack," just behind Jim who was on "point", that is, first in line.

Brownwood was down on the trail. He wasn't making any sound at all.

I hit the dirt and readied my M16 for action. After a minute or two, there were no incoming rounds, so I got up and ran over to Brownwood.

There were flecks of shaving cream and blood everywhere. He looked sort of crumpled like a rag doll that had been thrown into the corner of a child's bedroom.

Sergeant Speer, the company command NCO, [noncommissioned officer], was with us and was walking about fifteen yards behind Brownwood. He was screaming with pain.

A smoke grenade that was attached to Sergeant Speer's flack jacket had been set off and a piece of his shoulder was missing. It looked like green smoke was pouring from his wounded shoulder, a very bizarre scene.

After reaching Brownwood, he looked right into my eyes and said, "Are you shitting me?"

All that I could say was, "No."

Brownwood had stepped on a pressure-release triggered booby trap that was buried under the trail. Jim and I had walked right over it. It works when someone steps on it which sets the trigger. When you release the pressure by stepping off of it, it detonates.

Tex said that sometimes you can feel and or hear the trap set, when that happens, you must not move until someone can dig around it and disarm it while you keep the pressure on the trigger with your foot.

Our radioman was calling for a "dust off." We got Brownwood and Sergeant Speer loaded onto the medical evacuation helicopter. That was the last time I saw either of them.

Brownwood had only three more days to serve in the field when he stepped on that booby trap.

I felt sad and sick for Brownwood and Sergeant Speer. I didn't want to see any more blood or wounds. Nor hear any more screams.

I thought back to my basic training brigade at Fort Lewis, Washington. After taking all of the tests, the cadre said I was eligible for every job the army offered. He handed me a long list of jobs and stations that I could chose from. I chose "data processing" and for overseas duty, Germany. Later the cadres told us that list was called the "dream sheet" and now I knew why.

As we continued our march, with two less grunts, I thought about Rob's departure. He looked ecstatic when he climbed aboard the resupply chopper and I envied him.

I felt very loaded down; not only with the many foreboding thoughts and the severe lack of sleep but mostly by the heavy combat load I was carrying, which must have weighed about eighty pounds.

I had packed too much ammo, figuring that I certainly never wanted to run out; two plastic quart size canteens of water, enough food for three days along with the many other combat necessities.

When we marched near some thick bushes, I tossed my gas mask into them. No one else was carrying one. I simply threw it away. Later I dropped some of the extra ammo into a stream we were fording. I rationalized that the enemy would not find it there.

I also jettisoned one of the canteens opting to refill from the many canals, rivers and streams located in our area of operations. We had been issued purification tablets that made the water taste like iodine and battery acid, so instead of using them, I would mix in a packet of "Kool Aid" to disguise the awful taste. Miraculously, I never got sick from drinking this repulsive brew.

We never reached the downed helicopter. The terrain was too difficult and we could not cover that much ground in so short a time.

It was nearly sunset when we finally arrived at our night ambush site. We placed some claymore mines and trip flares on our perimeter. The claymores and trip flares were positioned on likely avenues of approach for the long night ahead. Also, we always planned a retreat route in case we were overrun by the enemy during the night.

We were in what was referred to as "the Pineapple." The area was called this on account of the many pineapple fields that crazy quilted the landscape. Each was surrounded by dykes that were constructed during the French colonial days to facilitate irrigation. The tops of the dykes were used as trails and especially for the transport of product from the paddies. Everywhere else was dense with abundant, nearly impassable jungle.

The Pineapple was a short distance south and west of Saigon. It was used by the enemy as a sanctuary/staging area and as an approach route to Saigon, capital city of the Republic of South Vietnam.

The Colonel said that we would be staying in the Pineapple for about two weeks. After that we would stand down for Christmas.

Set an ambush, patrol to another ambush site, eat rations and pineapples, ambush, patrol, eat…on and on, day after day. The weeks went by. Wet all night, every night. A pair of dry socks were more precious than gold.

Every three to four days we were resupplied by helicopter. Mail also was delivered by the choppers. A letter from home could bring a few minutes of joy to this tortured land of death and destruction.

CHAPTER FOUR

CHRISTMAS AND NEW YEAR

"There is no instance of a country having benefited from prolonged warfare." Sun Tzu

Operations continued in the PINEAPLE. Sniper fire was received in two brigade areas. A riverine search found 17 AK47's, 69 rounds of B-40 rockets, 2,000 pounds of C4, eight shovels, a first aid box and a number of homemade booby traps. The cache was located so that it would be under water at high tide. Company B, Riverine also found three cases of C4, 25 booby traps, 100 electrical blasting caps, and 350 non-electrical blasting caps. Local patrols in the 3/7th's AO found two bunkers, two steel helmets, one canteen and one Chicom grenade. Sniping and harassing continued in the TN Buu area.

[Intelligence Summary, 199th Inf Bde {Sep} {Lt} INTSUM 54-69]

Christmas was just around the corner and word came that we would be going to Long Binh, our main brigade base, for rest and for a real Christmas dinner.

Until then, we were still in the "free fire" zone of the pineapple. This meant that we could shoot anything that moved, in any direction. I hadn't seen anyone but fellow grunts since that first day.

Set an ambush, patrol to another ambush site, eat rations and pineapples, ambush, patrol, eat…on and on, day after day after day. It went by. Wet all night, every night.

Getting three hours of sleep per day, when lucky. My feet felt like they were going to dissolve, melt right off of my ankles.

Mom sent me a large package of homemade brownies and a marine combat knife. The package came with our resupply chopper. The brownies were all gooey and melted from the heat. We always shared whatever we got in the mail, so the brownies were consumed in about two minutes.

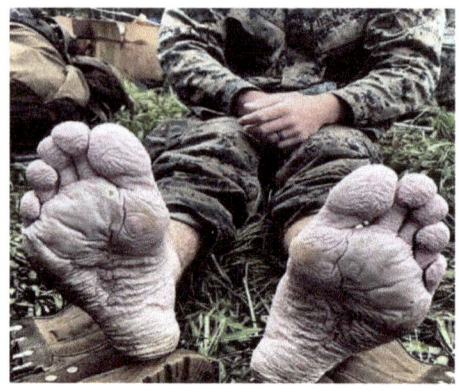

Finally a Chinook helicopter came to take us to Long Binh. Our headquarters, just a small part of this sprawling base, was called "Redcatcher" and we were called "Redcatchers."

My company was known as "Dakota" Company. We were the 5th Regiment of the 12th Infantry, which used to be known as "Red Warriors," a nickname that came from the American Indian War days, when the 12th Infantry fought the Modoc and Bannock Indians in California and Oregon. It was changed to "Redcatchers" for this war.

The motto of the 12th Infantry is, Ducti Amore Patriae, in English; "having been led by love of country." That of the 199th Light Infantry Brigade is; "Light, Swift, Accurate." The 199th was the only brigade constructed specifically for the Vietnam War. We were operating just like the enemy, at least in theory.

We finally got word that Brownwood had been sent to a hospital in Japan. He was going to be alright after a long recuperation.

Mike Donnelly, a new replacement for the squad arrived looking clean, fresh, well fed and rested.

At Long Binh we relaxed, exchanged our filthy clothes for freshly laundered ones, took cold showers, got shaves and haircuts, drank cold sodas or beer, ate hot chow from the mess hall and watched movies after dark.

"The Graduate" was showing and few of us wanted to miss it. When Dustin Hoffman drove the wrong way through the Gaviota tunnel, [on his way to Santa Barbara], from Berkeley, I had to laugh out loud while the guys nearby gave me a strange look since they had no idea what I was laughing at.

Long Binh was much like a huge city, having many of the comforts of home.

I ate lunch at the snack bar which looked like a "Dairy Queen." After the movie, we smoked pot and listened to incoming rockets, not wanting to hunker down in one of the many sandbagged bunkers on base.

At this time in the war, Long Binh was the largest military base in the world. There were miles and miles of military equipment, row after endlessly long row of trucks, helicopters, storage containers, all baking in the blistering Vietnamese sunshine.

Christmas dinner was a welcome treat after eating LRRPs for weeks, roast turkey with all the side dishes and trimmings and it was hot!

Each of us was given gift packets of writing paper, pencils, candy, and so on from a second grade class in Pittsburgh. I really appreciated the small package of Kleenex which made excellent toilet paper.

Next morning, I was able to squeeze aboard a truck that was heading for the Bob Hope show with Ann Margaret at Bien Hoa, about ten miles from Long Binh. I was told that we grunts weren't allowed to go, but I went anyway.

At the show, the dignitaries and high officers of course, had already taken the best seats, close to the stage. The rest of us were seated very far back and out along the sides. We could barely see the stage and we weren't laughing at Bob Hope's jokes. When the ABC camera panned our way, we hand signaled the peace sign or the "bird".

New Year's Eve, we were back on ambush in the Pineapple. My feet were actually dry. It wasn't raining and we hadn't crossed any rivers that day. The night sky was filled with billions of stars. My thoughts were of a carefree, last second takeoff on an early morning, head high, winter wave at Rincon, sea spray from the lip raining down on the paddlers who had just scrambled over the shoulder of the peak helped by a push from the warm Santa Ana offshore breeze.

In my mind I threw a huge cut back, turned off the bottom of the wave, scooted back to the top and stepped forward on the board, riding the nose until the wave forced me to back peddle, drop to the bottom, then shoot again to the top, kicking out with a flyaway as the entire wave crashed over and ended its life on the rocky beach with a loud hiss.

Then Trish was holding me tightly in her arms, we were dancing and hugging at the "Doors" concert one warm evening in Santa Barbara. Laughing and kissing, hugging and smiling. Our love would last forever, or at least until I had to report to the army.

Both of us were "military brats." Our fathers were in the Air Force which had been the Army Air Corps until the Air Force was established in 1947.

I was born in a US Army hospital in Nuremberg, Germany, a few years after World War Two ended. She was born in Ohio at about the same time.

Here I was guarding a piece of Vietnamese jungle not knowing why, as 1969 arrived.

It was my turn to sleep, so I awakened Tex and passed him the wristwatch.

"Happy new year" I whispered.

"Happy new year," Tex mumbled as he sat upright.

Lying down, I pulled the poncho liner over me and was immediately asleep. After a while, the tide came in and we were all soaked, shoulders to toes.

"The wind doesn't blow in Vietnam, it SUCKS!" said our new squad leader, Tony Russell.

Set an ambush, patrol to another ambush site, eat rations and pineapples, ambush, patrol, eat…on and on, day after day after day.

CHAPTER FIVE

TET 1969

On the Job Training

"Come you masters of war

You that build all the guns

You that build the death planes

You that build the big bombs

You that hide behind walls

You that hide behind desks

I just want you to know I can see through your masks."

Bob Dylan

Operations continued in the PINEAPPLE with three companies conducting star team interdiction operations. Results: 1 US KIA (Chicom Booby trap). Two VC camps were located with the usual miscellaneous items. A small boy was apprehended while flying a kite. Four other people were also apprehended and evacuated for questioning. The kite was thought to be a signal for the VC.

The week of 5-11 January 1969, included a contact with the enemy which produced one of the most serious losses of equipment and personnel during the quarter.

[Intelligence Summary, 199th Inf Bde {Sep} {Lt} INTSUM 54-69]

Tet, the lunar New Year, is the most important holiday in Vietnam. It is celebrated somewhat like our Fourth of July, with fireworks, parties, and vacations, lots of good cheer, food and drink. This was also a time for the enemy to campaign hard against us. Tet begins on the first day of the first month of the Chinese calendar, around late January or early February.

Arriving with the resupply chopper was a letter from an old friend and fellow surfer. Mickey told me about the massive oil spill in Santa Barbara. An environmental nightmare was occurring at home. The incoming tides brought the corpses of fish, sea birds, seals and dolphins to my favorite beaches, which were now covered with a blanket of thick, black, sticky crude oil.

It seemed that even at the beaches where I had spent so many joyful and carefree youthful days, things had become very hostile.

At the Paris peace talks, they were arguing over the shape of the table at which they would sit.

During Tet, 1968, the most famous attacks of the war were conducted against American installations and many of the cities of South Vietnam. The enemy had even occupied the American embassy in Saigon until routed by a counter attack.

In our area of operations, we mostly battled with the Viet Cong. They were referred to as "Victor Charlie" or simply as Charlie, Charles or Chuck.

Charlie paid a steep price for attacking head on. They lost thousands of their troops while we Americans lost hundreds.

Regardless, the enemy did show that he could mount major attacks against us, just as the theater commander, General Westmoreland back home said; "He had seen light at the end of the tunnel" regarding our war in Vietnam.

Charlie had proven that Westmoreland's light wasn't at the end of any tunnels in Vietnam, where there was only more death and destruction.

Militarily the attacks were disastrous for the enemy but they were a psychological victory considering their coordination, ferocity and duration which obviously contradicted the phony good news being spread at the time by some American commanders, the media and others.

Newsman Walter Cronkite pronounced the war a "stalemate" on television at this point and Americans tended to believe him and not General Westmoreland.

The enemy decided to return to classic guerrilla tactics for Tet 1969. Hit and run ambushes, hidden booby traps and snipers insured that many Americans would become casualties while limiting that of their own.

Our feet, due to being constantly wet, were in very bad shape. The skin became softer and softer, the pores opened up and the skin could be pulled off with our fingers. This was called "immersion foot."

Tony said our feet needed to be dried out, so we were finally on our way back to the fire support base where we would lay around with our feet in the sunshine at the "dry out" bunkers.

He was transferred from first platoon to replace Brownwood and only had three more months before his combat tour would end. Tony was of average build, black hair, strong brown eyes, serious but quick to smile…a combat veteran who had leaned how to survive on the job in the killing fields of Vietnam.

Tony wrote poetry in a tiny notebook at every opportunity, when things slowed down. He kept it in his helmet band or in his top jungle shirt pocket depending on whether we were crossing rivers or on dryer ground.

Tony was a good talker, too. He wanted to make it through this long, sad ordeal and he wanted all of us to survive also.

Tony was willing to teach me everything he had learned in Vietnam. I was a hungry student and a fast learner.

At our fire support base, which was about ten miles southwest of Saigon, my squad occupied the corner closest to the river which ran by us and under a traffic bridge. We had three sandbagged fighting and sleeping bunkers that were located directly on the perimeter. Behind us and towards center base, there was an old French fort with a tower where we had positioned a fifty caliber machine gun. It was on top of the tower where it had the largest field of fire. A starlight scope was mounted on the machine gun for night vision.

Next to our fire support base, [FSB], and in the direction of Saigon was a tiny Catholic village. The church was bombed and broken. It had no roof and was now just a hollow red brick shell.

Running through the village and our fire support base was the road from Saigon to My Tho, and places further south in the Mekong Delta.

The dry out bunkers were not on the perimeter. They were located on somewhat higher ground, not far from our ammo dump. We could go there, take our boots off, eat, write, read, talk or just sleep, all with our feet in the sun, of course. Also, since our feet were in such bad condition, usually we could not be tasked to do any of the many chores associated with running the FSB, the worst of which was "burning shit."

There was no plumbing, no baths, toilets, sinks or faucets. To defecate, we used wooden out houses which could seat four people at a time. The feces dropped through the hole we sat over and were collected in fifty gallon drums. When the drums were half filled, they would be removed by one of us, gasoline or diesel added and stirred in with a broom handle. Then it was ignited and continually stirred until it all burned away.

For urinating, we had "piss tubes." A length of metal pipe about the circumference of a chain link fence post was buried deeply into the ground. One stood above it and urinated into the small, exposed open end.

We were talking and enjoying the sunshine on our feet when "Top," the first sergeant, came over asking for volunteers. Top was a combat veteran of the Korean War, an army "lifer."

I silently back crawled into a bunker attempting to hide. Top saw me though. He told Tex and me to go down to the riverbank.

"I want you two to learn to drive the airboats, now!"

We would be taking out the night's ambushes in them.

Top ignored our protests regarding foot problems. Tex and I put our boots on and headed over to the river where the airboats were docked.

Airboats were small, flat bottomed, fiberglass watercraft propelled by a large rear mounted fan. They were used to navigate swamps and shallow water where other, propeller driven boats could not operate.

Sergeant Mills selected one and started the fan motor. Tex wanted to drive first, so we climbed aboard and sped off into the jungle.

Downstream we cruised for quite a ways. Tex was having fun as if we were on some friendly creek in Texas when we heard shots fired from the jungle nearby. One of the bullets struck the boat but we were unhurt. Small shards of fiberglass hit our legs and were deflected by our jungle pants.

Tex applied full throttle all the way back to our FSB and then it was my turn to drive.

While I was driving, the cage that enclosed and protected our propeller hit a tree branch that hung low over the river. The airboat stopped completely and it took us some time to regain control. After what seemed like a small eternity, we zoomed away and back to the fire base again. Now we were both official airboat drivers.

Walking back to the dry out bunkers, we both had a good laugh at our escapes from the ever present jungle dangers. Our good humor didn't last very long. Tony told us that we had to go on another ambush ourselves. Even though we were supposed to be drying and resting from the Pineapple, the Colonel was worried because of the coming Tet holidays which usually were a time for the enemy to attack us.

The plan was to take a squad of ARVNs [Army of the Republic of Vietnam, pronounced, "Arvins"], with us. There were eight of them packed and ready to go. We were to patrol to the ambush site near the river and about a half mile from the southeast corner of the fire base.

The colonel wanted this to be a "by-the-book" ambush, so he inspected us and told us to leave our cigarettes behind. We weren't supposed to smoke while on ambushes. The colonel watched as we put our cigarettes in the bunkers for safe keeping.

Once the colonel was satisfied, he walked back to his command bunker. Dupree got his portable record player, an album by Marvin Gaye but Tony told him to leave it behind this time. A few of us retrieved our contraband smokes, linked up with the ARVNs and headed out of the perimeter.

It was almost sunset by the time we reached the ambush site. Nearby was an old abandoned barn-like building. We set our ambush between it and the river. There was an empty fifty gallon drum there, so I sat down leaning back against it.

We talked in whispers while passing a single cigarette around. Tony was messing with our PRC 25 radio when the sky directly above us suddenly became brightly lit by a single exploding, white phosphorus, "WP" artillery round.

Tony called the command post radioman and was just receiving an answer when a second "WP" round exploded overhead. "WPs" were used as "marker" rounds to direct and position "HEs", that is, high explosive shells.

"Make that two "willy peters," marking our position," Tony was saying.

"Ignore those rounds," was the reply.

When five airburst "HE" rounds detonated in rapid succession above us, we found that they were impossible to ignore. I wrapped myself around the bottom of that fifty gallon drum as low to the ground as possible, trying to gain some protection from the flying shrapnel which was buzzing around us like a swarm of angry wasps.

As metal shards sung and whistled through the air, everything appeared totally hopeless to me. I had never been so scared and there was absolutely nothing any of us could do about it. As I clung to my M16 rifle, I thought I was about to die.

Once the barrage stopped and we all had escaped injury, Tony got back on the radio.

"We just took five "HE" rounds over our position, no one was hurt, request permission to move our ambush site now."

"Those were all "short rounds," permission denied, hold your ground," came the colonel's reply.

"Short round" was military speak for artillery shells that detonate before reaching their intended target.

We were all shaken, stunned and our ears were ringing like fire alarms due to the noise of the exploding artillery rounds.

"It don't mean nothin," Dupree complained.

The "Arvins" were gone. They had packed up their gear and marched back to the Catholic village near our fire base without saying anything to us.

It was unbelievable that none of us were hurt. Our minds were raging with a gut wrenching, profound anger that was never forgotten at this near death experience generated by our own artillery, called, "friendly fire." I was very glad to leave that ambush site, alive at dawn next morning.

The dry out bunkers were good to return to. The next few evenings, Tex and I took out many ambush teams in the airboats without incident. We drivers always returned alone at dusk after deploying ambush teams and went back solo in the morning to pick the teams up for the trip to our FSB.

Mike was twenty-two, older than most draftee's. He had been in Thailand for two years with the Peace Corps. When he returned home, the draft notice was waiting for him. So here he was with us Redcatchers working for the "war corps."

Top ordered Tex and me to teach Mike to drive airboats. We needed more drivers to take out and bring in ambush teams.

Mike mastered driving the air boats quickly and began taking out the teams that evening.

Next morning he was bringing a team back when we could hear AK47s, the enemies' rifles, firing in the distance. It sounded pretty bad for Mike. Counter ambushes on our airboats were par for the course.

After the firing died out, we could barely hear Mike's motor still running and becoming ever louder, as the moments passed. Then we could see Mike's boat coming towards us in the distance. As his image grew larger and larger, I was feeling somewhat relieved.

We ran over as Mike docked his boat. He was shaking and he looked very pale, blood was dripping from his mouth. No one else was injured.

"Doc" Wayne, one of our medics, examined Mike then said, "It looks like a round creased his lower lip."

We knew where the sniper was aiming. Mike had used some of his good luck.

I decided to start carrying a rabbit's foot.

CHAPTER SIX

SHORT-TIME CALENDARS

"Never think that war, no matter how necessary, nor how justified, is not a crime."—*Ernest Hemingway*

Seventeen miles west of Saigon, Delta Co. 5th Bn. 12th Inf engaged and killed one Viet Cong and destroyed 11 bunkers and one booby trap.

[From 199th LIB Summaries]

All of us had steel helmets and camouflaged helmet covers to protect our heads. We also had three hundred and sixty-five days to serve in Vietnam. We drew "short time" calendars on the helmet covers and crossed off the months as they crawled by. My helmet had only December crossed out, eleven more to go.

Some drew other things on their helmet covers, peace signs, nicknames, girl friends' names, hometown and etc.

I often carried a letter from home inside of mine with a pack of cigarettes held in the helmet band which was wrapped around the outside like a large rubber band. That kept the cigarettes dry when we forded streams.

Each day as the sun began setting, I would put a bottle of insect repellent in the helmet band for quick access. As the mosquitoes attacked in force, I'd roll my sleeves down, button them and then button my shirt to the neck and apply the repellant to my hands and face.

Set an ambush, patrol to another ambush site; eat rations and pineapples, ambush, patrol, cross a river, on and on, day after day.

We were on the trail of the enemy when we came to a small clearing with signs that the enemy had just left. Warm rice was still in the pots they had left behind in their haste. An empty, olive drab, C-ration can contained a booby trapped hand grenade.

On we marched until a Chinook helicopter, [we called them, "shit hooks"] appeared to transport us back to the FSB. The wind generated by the rotor blades blew tiny sticks, pieces of grass and dust into us as we loaded as fast as possible through the large open door at its rear.

I now carried a lot less ammo and food into the field. I hardly ever used any of the ammo, so I was hauling about half as much as before. I carried more hand grenades, called "frags" though.

Also, I carried a small AM/Fm radio that I had purchased at the PX, [Post Exchange] in Saigon and a large marine combat knife that I had received from my parents in the mail.

At the PX, I also bought some captain's insignia in case I was captured by the enemy. I figured that if they found the insignia on me, they might actually keep me alive longer to try and extract information from me.

During the entire war, any of us grunts that were captured were executed immediately by the enemy. No one under the rank of sergeant returned with the American prisoners of war after the U.S. military finally left Vietnam.

David Garcia arrived as a replacement; he was from Puerto Rico and spoke no English, but could understand it when spoken to, like Pappy. He was a great guy and would do anything we asked of him.

One evening my squad went on an ambush from our FSB and was ordered to take a Chieu Hoi along. Chieu Hoi's were also called, "Kit Carson scouts." We didn't want to take him, since we trusted none of the Vietnamese. Chieu Hoi's were soldiers that had changed sides for any number of reasons.

So we kept him in front of us, walking point. When we reached the ambush site just before dark, we set up the trip flares and David took out a claymore to set it up to our front. He had to ford a small irrigation canal to set it up on the other side. The trip flares were put at both ends of the dyke, on our flanks.

As David was fording the canal on his return from positioning the claymore, the Chieu Hoi fired a burst of rounds from his M16 in David's direction.

All of us yelled at the Chieu Hoi to stop firing. Tex grabbed the Chieu Hoi's rifle. Then we heard David coming towards us through the water and miraculously, he was unhurt.

We all had our rifles pointed at the Chieu Hoi as he lay on the dyke trail. Tony got on the radio and told the Colonel that we were sending the Chieu Hoi back to the FSB alone. We were not about to spend the rest of the night with him.

The Colonel agreed with us and we sent him off into the night. We never saw that Chieu Hoi again.

Next day, after returning from the night ambush, the entire company formed together for an "Eagle Flight" into the "Plain of Reeds." We were to search for dead bodies, equipment and any signs of the enemy. The area had been "carpet bombed" last night by the air force flying out of Thailand.

"Eagle Flights" were helicopter rides into remote, inaccessible terrain that could not be reached by any other means at our disposal or to surprise the enemy with our sudden assaults from the air. Six of us would sit shoulder to shoulder, face to face, inside the choppers, on two low benches. Five to ten "birds" would be flying in the formation, depending on the mission.

At times, we would sit on our helmets to keep the shrapnel generated by incoming bullets from hitting us. A gunner was perched at each open door to prepare the LZ, [landing zone], with his swivel mounted M60 machine gun to return any fire and to cover us as we leapt out after descending.

The "Plain of Reeds" was a huge area of desolate, bomb cratered, water covered wilderness marshland, with hundreds of rivers and streams spider webbing it.

As we approached our landing zone, the numerous clumps of very large reed plants that inhabited the place looked to me like massive sea urchin spines, sticking up from a surreal ocean bottom. Much of it was pockmarked and churned by the thousands of American bombs exploded there.

The choppers would or could not land nor even approach very close to the ground, so we all jumped at about eight feet above it. I landed in the mud which was up to my knees. I was hoping that no enemy was around and that we would not have to stay the night. The day was spent searching for signs of the enemy and fighting with the mud. We took a break for lunch but there was no dry place to sit down. I simply backed myself into a huge clump of reeds for a little support as I opened a can of peaches and drank from my canteen.

We found lots of tracks made by bare feet. Tiny bits and pieces of people and their clothing were scattered about from those who were unfortunate enough to be under the exploding five hundred pound bombs. I found some intact web gear that contained a beautifully engraved Chinese made oil can along with ammo filled magazines for an AK47.

The web gear looked handmade with thick, cotton canvas material, hand carved bone buttons, strong stitching and very unlike the cheap, flimsy, machine made bandoliers we were issued.

I thought I would keep the oil can as a souvenir, but the Captain wanted it and took it from me, along with the web gear and AK magazines.

All of us were very glad to see the choppers come in that evening to take us away from this hell on earth.

CHAPTER SEVEN

PINEAPPLE AGAIN

"The belief in the possibility of a short decisive war appears to be one of the most ancient and dangerous of human illusions."—Robert Lynd

Brigade elements with help from the 9th Inf Div tightened the cordon established yesterday around an unknown-size enemy force 9 miles north of Tan An.

[From 199th LIB Summaries]

(c) Riot Control Agent: 1-30 February, thirteen persistant CS operations were conducted within the 199th Inf Bde AO. Two of the operations were aerial and eleven were ground operations. The aerial CS operations were flown in a UH1-D helicopter provided by the 199th Brigade Aviation Section. The Persistant CS was used to cover canal lines and areas of suspected enemy concentrations along the Kinh Cau An Ha Canal. 480 pounds of CS were expended during the operation. The 8 pound packs of CS were wrapped with detonation cord with 8 second delay blaster being used to destruct the pack. The missions were flown at 100 feet, at 50 knots so as to give good area coverage. The ground operations consisted of emplacing 7920 pounds of CS along canal lines and known areas of enemy activity at the following locations: "Five fingers" area, Nuog

Long River, Ong Hen Canal, Ong Com Canal, and Ong Do Canal. The CS munitions now used in support of the 199th Inf Bde are E-158 CS Cluster, E-8 CS Rocket Launchers, M-7 CS Hand Grenades, and 55 gallon drums of bulk CS. These munitions are maintained in a constant state of readiness for instantaneous support of the brigade.

[Intelligence Summary, 199th Inf Bde {Sep} {Lt} INTSUM 54-69]

Typically, there were three or four of us on the march. We would construct an ambush just before the sun set and be in this ambush site all night. At sunrise we would eat rations, drink instant coffee and pack our gear, then move out for the day's combat patrol and more ambushes.

Claymores were stuck in the ground on the perimeter of our position, upon small metal legs. On the side that faced the enemy was printed, "FRONT TOWARD ENEMY." A wire was strung from the mine back to our ambush site. They were detonated with a hand held triggering device.

Occasionally the enemy would sneak up to our claymore mines at night and reverse their position, then make some noise in an attempt to trick us into to blowing ourselves away. Because of this trick, I would never detonate a claymore mine, no way!

Whenever possible, the enemy would note our location and booby trap all of the egresses leading from our ambush site. So, on far too many occasions as we moved from an all night ambush site, the horrible sound of an explosion would shatter the morning calm and welcome us to the day's march. We would call for a "dust off," [helicopter medical evacuation] on our PRC 25 radio.

At the sound of the approaching medevac, we would "pop" colored smoke with a smoke grenade to mark the LZ. The chopper would land and we would load the wounded or dead victim into the chopper then be on our sad and weary, but perhaps wiser way.

The morning that Jim was wounded, I decided not to look at any more of our casualties unless I absolutely had to. This was my way of attempting to remain sane. If I didn't look, perhaps I would not have to feel any more pain nor anger.

The pain, anger and the profound weariness overwhelmed me after Jim was "dusted off." I felt that I was probably next, and then alternately, I felt invincible.

As my "star team" moved out, this time I decided not to go. I stayed down prone and told the others just to let me rest. Death seemed like a welcome relief from my weariness, anger and pain. Now I wanted to die simply to rest from this madness.

"Go on without me; leave me alone, I don't want to go any farther."

"Saddle up, we're moving out!" Tony yelled at me.

My squad was moving out without me. I continued to lay there on the ground for a few minutes and then it passed. The only time in my life that I felt like dying, giving it all up, passed, never to return.

I was walking point now days. The rate of attrition demanded it and I felt safer in front, leading the way. Since I was older, 21, when most of the guys were 18 and 19, some of them began calling me "Pappy".

While walking point, I always attempted to walk wherever I thought the enemy would determine that we would not walk. It was important to think like the enemy to survive. This often meant that I would have to break trail with a machete. Of course this also meant that we could not move very fast, but to me, a slower pace was preferable compared to being blown away by a booby trap or walking into the kill zone of an enemy ambush.

On point I would carefully look for anything out of place or different from the normal surroundings. Tracks, a broken twig, grass or bushes bent over where it should not be…any signs, sounds or smells of the enemy are some examples.

When complaints were aimed at me, I simply asked the complainer if he wanted to exchange positions on the march and that would end the discussion.

After patrolling for what seemed like days, we found our designated ambush site just after sunset. It was a good site, because we spent the night without being immersed by the incoming tides of the Mekong Delta and there was no enemy action to deal with.

When the sun came up, we could see that we were on high ground between a wide river and a small stream. They intersected at nearly right angles and we had camped at that intersection. We radioed in our "sit rep," [situation report] and were ordered to hold our position to become a blocking force.

Some elements of the Ninth Division that were located just south of us had encountered an enemy patrol and they were chasing them directly towards us. The Ninth Division was conducting "Operation Speedy Express" at this time. "Speedy Express" was the largest killing operation of the entire war as the vast majority of the Vietnamese casualties had no weapons on them. I learned this only after I returned to the United States as we were told little or nothing while in the field. Most Americans have never heard of this operation and the Army prefers to keep it that way.

We busied ourselves with setting up an ambush for the anticipated action. Our fields of fire aimed in the direction from which they would be coming. We all faced away from the intersecting waterways.

About a half mile away, down the river and on the same side as we were on was a second ambush site. It was manned by another of our "star" teams. They had a medic with them also. Many of our medics carried rifles as well as all of their medical gear.

We waited silently for an hour or so. Tony, looking through the field glasses spotted a squad of enemy soldiers walking out of the tree line about a mile from us. They were advancing directly towards our sister ambush team up the river.

Time passed like cold honey being poured from a jar. I secretly hoped that the enemy would change direction and avoid our bullets.

We all heard an M16 fire from our sister ambush team and this single shot gave away their position causing the enemy to turn back towards the tree line and away from our waiting ambush teams.

The Colonel wasn't happy that our medic had fired his rifle which warned the enemy. I assumed that "Doc" [what we called all of our medics] didn't want to patch any wounds or put anyone on a dust off chopper this morning.

The enemy patrol moved within the tree line. The colonel decided to have CS gas dropped on them to flush them out. This gas irritated with an itchy, burning sensation all skin and eyes that it came in contact with and if breathed in, would cause severe nausea and profuse sweating from every pore.

Ironically, soon after the gas was dropped the breeze carried it directly into our ambush site. Since none of us carried gas masks, we all grabbed our towels and wet them in the river. We wrapped them around our faces to breathe through and stayed as low as possible to the earth. This saved us from being debilitated by the noxious gas. I figured the enemy knew the same tricks, of course.

The enemy patrol escaped.

Doc later told us; "I'm sick of patching guys up for no good reason, it don't mean nothin."

After getting our gear together, we were off for another combat patrol along the riverbank. As we walked along the river behind a screen of trees and bushes, we heard the sound of a swift boat motor. The U.S. Navy used these small, fast boats to patrol the rivers. Suddenly the boat opened fire and a fifty caliber machine gun round smacked into the mud at my feet. The hole it made was about the size of a man's fist.

I dived down behind a small rise in the ground thinking the next bullet might have my name on it. Our RTO [radio telephone operator] called the swift boat and they said that they were taking some target practice and that they didn't know we were in the way.

"Oops, sorry," was their apology as they sped away from us.

So far I have been fired on by other Americans far more than by the enemy. Fire from one's allies was called "friendly fire" even though it could kill or main you just as efficiently as any barrage from the enemy. I was learning to fear everybody, including the "friendlies."

Set an ambush, patrol to another ambush site; eat rations and pineapples, ambush, patrol, cross a river, on and on, day after day.

We were moving through very thick jungle area that had signs written in Vietnamese, posted in some of the trees warning of booby traps. We were looking for a good ambush site. If we kept walking, someone would surely be blown away by one of the traps, some of which were in small holes about the size of one's feet. At the bottom would be sharpened bamboo stakes with human excrement smeared on the tips to insure a very nasty infection.

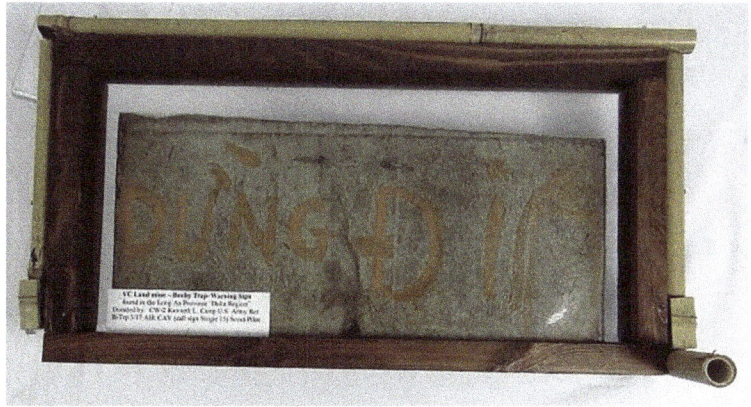

Our orders were to keep patrolling and to blow any enemy bunkers that we happened to come upon. This particular area had lots of enemy bunkers that we naturally tried to stay away from. Our only rational task was to try to survive this war as best we could. But the colonel was on the radio ordering us to blow bunkers.

Tony said we should move as little as possible and throw hand grenades into the creek because on the radio this sounded exactly like bunkers being blown up.

Calling in our sit reps hourly we reported many bunkers being blown, which the Colonel could hear in the background. Thus, we all made it through another day without any casualties among us.

CHAPTER EIGHT

A COMPANY SWEEP

"There never was a good war or a bad peace."—Benjamin Franklin

The brigade, continuing under the operational control (OPCON) of Capital Military Assistance Command (CMAC) participated in Operation TOAN THANG II and III in AO Jane were directed primarily against traditional base camps and staging areas of the 308th and 6th Local Force Battalions. Objectives were to preempt theses areas from use, interdict lines of communications and prevent enemy rocket/mortar and ground attacks against Saigon. Operations in the Pineapple were designed to locate VC sites and disrupt supply operations. All elements of the brigade continued aggressive offensive operations and night ambushes on all likely western and southwestern land and water approaches into Saigon.

[Intelligence Summary, 199th Inf Bde {Sep} {Lt} INTSUM 54-69]

Upon linking up with the other platoons in my company, we were to sweep through an area of higher ground. We walked through huge stands of bamboo and nipa palm, and the shade cast by larger trees offered welcome relief from the relentless heat.

Coming to a small clearing, someone noticed an artillery shell that appeared to be hanging high up in the branches of a very tall tree.

Captain Braden looked at me and said, "Go check out that tree, Private."

"Why don't we all get back from it and then shoot it out of the tree?" I asked.

"You fucking pussy." The captain said looking disgusted.

Captain Braden's RTO then said; "I wouldn't go near that tree, Cap, why don't we just recon it with M16 fire?" "Negative, I'm going to have a look-see."

Then the Captain walked over to the tree in question. As soon as he was almost directly under the shell, it exploded.

The medevac chopper was already on its way. Our ears were ringing from the blast. I could not believe how stupid the captain was and now he was nearly dead. There was nothing our medic could do for him. We lost a lot of officers in a similar fashion.

I slept with my boots on, feet in the water that night. I wanted my feet to deteriorate faster thinking that might get me out of this horror a little sooner. Marijuana cigarettes were passed around and smoked by a few of us.

When morning arrived, word came that we were to be airlifted out so we needed to hump over to the designated LZ. Lieutenant Calder ordered me to stay behind, wait for 30 minutes and then blow up all of our trash and debris. This was done so that the enemy could not use anything that we left behind. If any enemy units were around and heard the noise, they would only ambush me, not the entire company.

After exploding the trash, I was to track and follow my unit through the jungle to rejoin them at the LZ. So I waited a half hour, after all of the others departed. I then blew up the trash with a large chunk of C4 that I formed around a blasting cap that was used as a detonator. Then I walked as fast and as quietly as possible with the load I was carrying, scared out of my wits and was very relieved when I finally caught up.

While we waited for the choppers to arrive, most everyone was talking about where we would be going next. I was extremely tired all of the time. We were only getting about three hours of rest per day. I really needed some decent sleep.

Everything that had happened in my life before arriving in Vietnam seemed like ancient history now, a vague, very distant dream. My reality was to find ways to remain alive.

One way was almost always wearing my helmet and flack jacket, regardless of the extremely hot weather. Others were walking point or drag to stay away from the main body of a formation which makes the most lucrative target, staying off of trails which were prime areas for booby traps and staying awake as much as possible.

Some of the guys were saying that we might eventually be moving north to Cu Chi or maybe over to a place called "Black Horse." Wherever we would be going, my hope was that it would be a lot safer and dryer than in the Pineapple.

CHAPTER NINE

FISHNET FACTORY

"Men will not fight and die without knowing what they are fighting and dying for."—*General Douglas MacArthur*

5\12 Infantry elements were inserted west of the area where contact was made on 23 Jan, as a complementary action, with negative results.

[Intelligence Summary, 199th Inf Bde {Sep} {Lt} INTSUM 54-69]

An old fishnet factory is where our battalion headquarters was located. It was just on the outskirts of Saigon, on about four square blocks of land and partially enclosed by a high concrete block wall that had many large holes blown in it from prior enemy attacks. We had machine gun emplacements where the holes were and concertina wire outside and beyond them.

Next to the factory but in the same compound was the owner's attractive, well built two story concrete and stucco home. My squad was ordered to camp on the flat, low walled roof so as to have a good view of the entire perimeter. This was a great place for the night, no tide nor ambushes.

We knocked on the door and an elderly, well dressed Vietnamese woman answered. Since we spoke no Vietnamese and she spoke no English, we indicated with hand signs that we needed entry through her house to the roof. She opened the door and indicated that we could go wherever we wanted.

I felt sorry for her that we were tramping through her home with our dirty boots. We were probably messing up her life more than anything else. She looked worried.

While situating ourselves on the roof and scouting our fields of fire, Tex mentioned that there were "short time" girls just outside the wire, in back of the compound.

"All we have to do is scoot through the wire later on."

Fishnet was where our battalion artillery was located, also. There were a lot of missions being fired that afternoon. It was so loud that napping was impossible for me. Sleep was an elusive, delicious, longed for luxury that I was consistently denied.

Where fishnets were once fabricated, we now had our troops and their rear echelon supporters talking, sleeping, eating, cleaning and restoring various weapons, giving and taking orders, coming and going.

The rows of bulky, antiquated machines, sulking hulks of rusted and cobwebbed metal once furiously busy, industriously working to make fishnets for peasant fishermen were sitting quietly now as though they were all stoically waiting for the madness to end so they could get back to work.

I received orders over our radio to relieve the guard at the front gate for two hours, so I got my rifle and reported there.

The gate was a large, red and white painted wooden bar that I was to open and close for the vehicle traffic as it came and went. There was also a small plywood guard shack to sit in that provided shade from the sweltering, relentless sunshine.

From the guard shack I saw a teenaged girl riding a bicycle, wearing the traditional white dress with slits on the sides peddling along in the heavy, chaotic traffic. She was going home from school, I imagined.

A man on a fast moving motor scooter plowed into her bike. She was catapulted into the air landing head first on the pavement as her legs began kicking at the air. The motor scooter kept on going and no one stopped to help her.

My stomach churned, my head felt dizzy as I forced myself to look away. I silently promised myself that I would never look at such a scene ever again.

When I finally looked again, the Vietnamese police had arrived and were clearing traffic for the ambulance.

I was relieved by the next guard just before sunset. I went to our roof to rest a little before chow time. There was hot chow at Fishnet, what a treat!

After eating, Tex and I walked to the rear corner of the compound where an M60 machine gun nest was positioned in one of the large holes in the surrounding wall.

We said hello to the troopers manning the gun as we climbed through an opening in the wire. They laughed and asked if we were going to see the "short time" girls. We laughed back at them.

After a short walk we came to a one room "hooch" with a roof of palm branches. The walls were made of flattened tin cans, wooden and cardboard boxes plus other scrounged materials. It had only one piece of furniture on the dirt floor. Positioned in the middle of the room was a wooden bed that had bamboo strips woven together as a kind of hammock mattress.

As if by magic two Vietnamese teenaged girls appeared. Tex talked with them awhile then asked me to keep guard as he went inside of the "hooch" with one of the girls.

After about fifteen minutes Tex walked out of the "hooch" with a very large grin on his face.

"Your turn."

I declined the invitation gracefully, concealing the fact that I was so tired and scared that I had no desire.

We walked back to Fishnet, ducking back through the same hole in the wall. The grunts on the machine gun laughed even louder this time as we walked by them.

The artillery continued firing most of the night and of course I had to pull my share of guard duty. Once again, I got very little sleep. I was extremely tired all of the time.

CHAPTER TEN

PARROT'S BEAK

"War is not an adventure. It is a disease. It is like typhus."—*Saint-Exupery*

In the PINEAPPLE, 5/12 Inf conducted a search in the area known as PARROT'S BEAK, and found three large sampans. In the 4/12 Inf's AO, one company conducted RIF and interdiction operations.

There were also routine search-patrols within the 4/12 and 5/12 AO's.

[Intelligence Summary, 199th Inf Bde {Sep} {Lt} INTSUM 54-69]

In the morning at chow, everyone was talking about where we would be going next. No one knew, of course. We never knew in advance, we only heard rumors.

Loading into the choppers, Tony said he thought we were heading west for the "Parrot's Beak," right on the border of South Vietnam and Cambodia. It was called this because the shape of the borderline on the map, which looked vaguely like the beak of a parrot.

The Eagle Flight to the "Parrot's Beak" was uneventful until we started descending on a patch of slightly higher ground, which was an ancient looking graveyard near a wide river. Some of the blackened, leafless, trees were still burning and smoking from the early morning artillery barrage that had prepared the area for our arrival.

Suddenly bullets were whizzing around us, some of them shot through the thin metal walls of the choppers. I jumped out and down as fast as I could. This was called a "hot LZ."

Fortunately, the bullets were coming from the other side of the river so it was nearly impossible for the enemy to actually hit any of us.

"So this is what a fire fight is like," I was thinking to myself.

Many of us began firing back, at will. I decided not to shoot my rifle since I could not see anything to fire at; might as well save the ammo just in case the attack worsened.

An hour or so passed with us pinned down when I saw a small rock hit on the ground near me. I thought nothing of it until another small stone glanced off of my helmet.

I rose up slightly to look around and saw Lieutenant Calder, who was laying prone about 30 feet from me, throw another piece of gravel my way. He was trying to signal me to fire my rifle and I ignored him.

Shortly after this, the firing thankfully ended.

Air strikes were called in since the river was too wide for us to ford. Our jets bombed and strafed the enemy positions. Tex said the jets were: "Bringing pee on Charlie."

When the air strikes ended, we saddled up and patrolled the rest of the day. Someone said that we were actually in Cambodia and that was supposed to be illegal.

"I don't see any welcome signs or fences," Doc Wayne offered. We had a good laugh.

Booby traps were everywhere. Luckily we made no further contact with the enemy and none of us were hurt.

We formed near another wide river to be picked up by "LCM" boats, [landing craft, medium], or "Mike boat." These boats were similar to those used on D-Day to land troops and equipment on the beaches of Normandy. They hit the beach, the front ramp swings down and we troops use the ramp to go ashore.

I hated the "LCMs." They traveled very slowly, made the noise of a street full of Mack trucks. We were sitting ducks for enemy ambushes while inside of them.

I would load on to these boats last and thus be the first one to run off the ramp, figuring to shorten the time that I, personally would be at increased risk. While in the boats we could not return fire effectively since we could not see well nor shoot with any accuracy over the armored walls. We preferred to be picked up by helicopters; they were much faster and far safer.

My entire platoon boarded one of the boats. We stacked all of our ammo and other equipment in the center of the deck. I would get into one of the front corners which afforded me armor protection on two sides. Many of the guys would take off their helmets and flack jackets for comfort. I almost always kept mine on for extra protection.

When the boat took us through narrows where the banks were very close together, we all really sweated it out.

Mike was trying to catch more of the cooling breeze by sitting on the top edge of one of the armored sidewalls. Suddenly he lost his balance and fell overboard into the water below. The propeller on the boat tended to suck everything down and into it, so Tex jumped over in an effort to help Mike. Others were yelling at the boat driver to turn the engine off.

I saw a rope that was rolled neatly, attached to the side of the boat and threw it over to them so that they both would not be sucked down. Tex caught hold of the rope with one hand and grabbed Mike, who was going under, with his other hand. Tony and others helped pull them from the water and we all had a great laugh when they both were hauled back inside.

After a lengthy "LCM" ride, we went ashore for our next mission. This was to set up a "blocking force," that is, become the "anvil" for a "hammer" unit. The hammer and anvil tactic involved one unit, the hammer, which would be on the march, forcing the enemy into our anvil, the stationary unit, for a shootout.

Some units of the Ninth Division were to chase the VC into our waiting kill zones. Lieutenant Calder told us to hurry and construct our fighting positions because he expected action very soon.

"Hurry up and wait" is what we called such orders.

This was a good place compared to many of the other ambush sites I had occupied so far. The ground was higher and dryer, large trees here and there, a somewhat cleared jungle area so that we could see to our front. We were afforded a little protection from a raised dyke trail that ran the length of our blocking force. We were in company strength, about thirty troopers, so I felt a bit safer also.

We excavated no foxholes, the ground was below sea level and any hole dug would quickly fill with water.

I figured this would be a good place to get some sleep since the terrain was dry and we were in forceful numbers. Funny cigarettes were passed by some, high and dry.

We worked out our guarding sequence for the night.

At sunup, some enemy troops did quietly approach our position. We saw them though, and after some shooting from both sides, they moved away from our guns, back in the direction from which they had come. They left two of their dead behind.

The Captain got on the "horn," what we called the PRC25 radio, and called for a tracker dog team to be helicoptered in to our position as well as a "dust off" for the casualties.

Twenty minutes later, in a tumult of purple smoke, flying dust, twigs, leaves and other debris, the dog team arrived. Two German shepherds with two handlers, along with the medevac chopper.

The Captain needed to task a squad to chase after the enemy through the jungle with the dog team leading the way. The dogs would often set off booby traps with their incessant running and sniffing, rendering working with them even more hazardous than usual for us grunts.

Cap looked at me first. I discreetly shook my head. I would not volunteer for what I considered a suicide mission.

Then he said, "Seidenberg, go with the dog team."

I told him; "You can't order me to commit suicide."

The Viet Cong would usually set booby traps along the way if followed. I knew this by now, intuitively as well as from first hand observation.

Survival was the fundamental mission: I didn't want to be a dead hero. I didn't want to see anyone else get hurt on account of our stupidity either.

Next the captain told Mike, who was sitting right next to me, to go along with three other grunts on the dog patrol. Mike and I had become fast friends. Mike got up and joined the dog patrol without saying a word. The rest of us remained in our blocking force positions.

After about half an hour, we heard a loud explosion, then the bad news came via our radio. One of the dogs had set off a booby trap and Mike had to be dusted off. I never saw Mike again; he died almost instantly from his wounds. The two dogs had been slightly injured also and were dusted off before Mike was.

I yelled at the captain, "It's criminal to dust off a dog before a human being."

"It cost more to train a dog than it does a grunt." The captain answered.

"It don't mean nothin," strolled through my mind.

Army officers use grunts like a carpenter uses nails.

I felt horrible for Mike, very sad and guilty, yet at the same time I was feeling strangely euphoric to be alive. Paradoxically mixed emotions came with the territory.

The Chinook choppers came to get us just ahead of sunset and I was very glad to be leaving that killing field.

CHAPTER ELEVEN

DRY OUT BUNKERS AGAIN

"For a Christian who believes in Jesus and his Gospel, war is an iniquity and a contradiction."—*Pope John XXIII*

5/12 Infantry continued operations in AO Swordfish III. A/D/5/12 Inf became OPCON to TF KAY for Operation STRANGLER II on 12 Feb.

[Intelligence Summary, 199th Inf Bde {Sep} {Lt} INTSUM 54-69]

Tex and I were talking about home and girlfriends, cars and sports, what we would do if we made it back to "the world." How we would love to have a cheeseburger, fries and a chocolate shake when the subject abruptly changed.

"Why do you want to kill people? I can't see any reason for doing so myself."

Tex didn't answer. He got up and walked towards the outhouse without saying word.

I decided to ask our new captain about the killing. Captain Williams had replaced Captain Braden. We went through a lot of captains.

It seemed to me that killing in cold blood ran counter to the Ten Commandments besides being morally wrong in my own heart. I still had no desire whatsoever to kill anyone. I shaved, straightened my dirty fatigues, adjusted my jungle hat and walked over to the command bunker.

Captain Williams said, "What's the problem, private?"

"I need to be transferred out of the infantry, I don't think I can do this work, I don't want to kill anyone."

"Seidenberg, I want you to talk with the chaplain," The captain answered.

"Yes sir."

I walked slowly back to the dry out bunkers, deep in thought.

At chow time, I wasn't very hungry, but I still went through the chow line at the mess tent and got a full plate of food. I walked over to where the Vietnamese children were scrounging through our garbage and gave them my paper plate of food.

It surprised me when, instead of digging right in, they ran with it back to their "Mamasan." She took it, divided it up into smaller portions and handed some to each child.

I walked back to the chow line to get a smaller portion of food, sat down and began eating with a plastic spoon.

A soft, mist-like rain began falling but the droplets looked brown and oily and there wasn't a cloud in the sky. I heard the sound of a small aircraft flying slowly above.

Tony said, "They are spraying for mosquitoes or that is "Agent Orange," weed killer."

"But that crap is going right into our food!"

"The brass says it's harmless to humans." Tony answered with an ironic laugh as he scribbled something in his ever present notebook.

I got up and dumped my food into a fifty gallon drum trash can that was placed nearby. Then I went back to the dry out bunkers to catch a little sleep.

"The chaplain is here to see you Pappy." Tex said while gently kicking my boot which was sticking slightly out of the bunker I was napping in.

The chaplain and I walked over to the quad fifties that were positioned on the perimeter for defense. We were alone; there was no one around these four fifty caliber machine guns that could be fired in unison like some hellish Gatling gun.

"What's the problem, son?"

"Sir, why are we here? No one, as yet, has explained this to me. I don't think I am cut out for this line of work. I don't want to pull the trigger, maybe I can't…I don't want to kill anyone."

The chaplain opened his Bible and read a few passages from it to me. He ended our chat by saying, "Son, you need to kill the enemies of God."

As the chaplain walked away, I thought that his was not a sufficient answer. Neither the chaplain nor I knew who or what God was or if God even existed; much less, who God's enemies were, if she, he or it indeed had any.

I was so tired that it was nearly impossible to think, I needed about a week of sleep just to feel rested again.

"We've got to have our teeth checked." Tex said with a wink.

"What…mine are OK."

"Naw, we both have toothaches, let's go see the Doc."

Our company doctor told us to get on the jeep that was conveniently about to leave for Third Field Hospital in Saigon, where there was a dental clinic.

CHAPTER TWELVE

A DENTAL APPOINTMENT

"War does not determine who is right—only who is left."—Bertrand Russell

5/12 Inf, continuing operations in AO Swordfish III, had several contacts with small groups of VC. 5/12 was OPCON to Bien Hoa Tactical Area Command (BHTAC) for operations in AO Hardcharger, effective 15 Feb. Operation STRANGLER II continued.

[Intelligence Summary, 199th Inf Bde {Sep} {Lt} INTSUM 54-69]

As our jeep rolled up to the gates of Third Field Hospital, we could see a dust off chopper landing inside of the compound. Tex and I checked our rifles with the MPs that were standing guard at the gate behind a sandbagged kiosk. We could see the wounded being off loaded onto gurneys and being rolled into the emergency ward. I forced myself to look away. I didn't want to see any more blood or broken men.

Tex told the main desk clerk that we were here to see a dentist about toothaches. The clerk told us that we would have to get into a very long line but that he would issue us bunks so that we could rest while waiting. We would have to spend the night; the earliest we could see a dentist would be tomorrow.

He held his nose while telling us we stunk of the field but that we could get brand new fatigues by going downstairs to the supply room and simply asking for them.

Saigon, at this time in the war, was "off limits" to all infantry personnel. I guessed that the brass didn't want us to frighten the city folks. It was more than obvious that we were both infantry because of our filthy clothes and very well worn boots.

After retrieving the new fatigues, we went to our bunks to change and began planning for our brief stay in Saigon. We emptied our pockets; between us we had eleven dollars in MPC [military payment certificates]. It was unlawful to have U.S. dollars or Vietnamese piasters.

We stuffed our dirty clothes into the lockers that were assigned to each bunk.

Firstly, to the baths, called the "Steam and Cream," this referred to bathing and shaving. It meant something even more refreshing to many of us.

The steaming hot water, real soap, thick clouds of steam and lovely, young rubdown girls were luxuries beyond belief.

"We need to make some money, we don't have enough to eat on or to party afterwards," Tex said.

With the five dollars MPC we had left, we bought a bottle of good scotch at the PX and sold it to a cab driver for a huge profit. The cab driver became our buyer as we worked our way up to a very nice electric fan.

Almost everything we bought at the PX was marked off of our ration cards. The cards are issued to every soldier to keep track of and limit our purchases.

While we were sitting inside the cab, I mentioned that I was a little worried about exhausting my ration card. The cabby reached under the front seat and pulled out a fat deck of ration cards wrapped in a thick rubber band.

"No sweat, Gee eye."

Back and forth we shopped at the PX until we worked our way up to an entire case of really good scotch whiskey. The cabby said that the Vietnamese pay the most for good scotch.

Now we had five hundred dollars. It had taken us about an hour to turn five dollars into five hundred dollars.

"To the steaks" Tex exclaimed.

The "Texas Steak House" was conveniently located not far from the "Steam and Cream." We both ordered beer, prime rib, salad and fries.

We walked a short distance to a multi storied hotel and paid for a four room suite. Tex told the "Papasan" that we wanted to party and that he should send all the girls he knows up to our suite.

The girls kept arriving the entire evening and we enjoyed the night as though we were rich tourists on an exotic vacation.

When two Australian ladies who lived nearby came in, we thought we were in heaven. We called them "round eyes" because of their Anglo heritage, their eyes were not almond shaped. Now we had girls that even spoke English.

Helen and Karen were in Vietnam entertaining the troops. They said that they were making good money. Bien Hoa was where they would be playing the next evening and they invited us to the show.

Back at Third Field Hospital next morning, we found out that the dentist still didn't have time to see us, so we would have to spend another night there. Neither of us were disappointed.

We wanted to go to the show at Bien Hoa Enlisted Men's Club, but how to get there? Bien Hoa was twenty perilous miles northeast of Saigon.

Fortunately we saw a parked jeep, not far from our hotel and the keys were in the ignition. The jeep was painted all white, meaning it belonged to the Saigon police department, the "white mice."

"Let's borrow it for the day," Tex said.

We hopped aboard and drove it all the way to Bien Hoa arriving just in time for the show. As the remaining daylight dwindled, a blast of artificial light along with the thick billowing haze of cigarette smoke greeted us from inside. In utter amazement, we stood for a while to get our bearings.

The Bien Hoa EM club was crammed full of rear echelon soldiers. They were talking, laughing and drinking booze all at the same time.

Karen and Helen saw us somehow and walked out to greet us and show us inside.

"We got to get out of this place, if it's the last thing we ever do," was screaming at us from the sound system.

Tex and I stayed for the entire show, the girls danced three sets, one every hour or so.

The fun ended around midnight, Tex and I said our goodbyes and with our jeep joined the last convoy leaving Bien Hoa heading back to Saigon.

Motoring along, things seemed almost normal when our jeep died; we pulled it over to the roadside as the long convoy continued to pass us by.

Neither of us had any weapons, other than the knives we always carried. As the last truck in the convoy faded into the night we were becoming a bit worried about being alone in "Indian Country."

At last we saw headlights coming towards us in the distance.

"Maybe we can hitch a ride?"

"Ya, alright," Tex answered.

When we were able to see the approaching vehicle better, we noticed it was a U.S. Army Military Police jeep and we figured that we were in deep trouble now.

The MPs were very gracious, though. We told them we had run out of gas and they said they would go get us some, and then return as soon as possible.

We were all alone again, very scared. About half an hour passed when we saw head lights in the distance once again. "Maybe the MPs are already coming back?" "I hope so," Tex whispered.

But we could hear loud engine noise…that of a large diesel motor.

When the truck finally came within view, we signaled it and were very happy when it pulled over. There was only the driver aboard and he was also very glad to see us.

We told him of our plight.

"Jump on up here, I'll ride you all the way to Saigon!" the driver beamed.

The white jeep was left by the roadside. I figured that the MPs would retrieve it, since we left the key in the ignition.

By the time we got back to our hotel, Helen and Karen were already asleep in their room. We saw them next morning and told them about our adventure with the convoy.

A good laugh was had by us all over breakfast of coffee, eggs, bacon and toast.

Afterwards, Tex and I said our goodbyes then headed back to Third Field Hospital for our dental appointments.

When we saw the MPs manning the sandbagged guard post, Tex said; "We better get our rifles and head back to Kathy, before Top decides that we are AWOL."

Most of our fire support and forward operating bases [FSB and FOB], were named after ladies.

A truck was going our way, so we jumped on it.

CHAPTER THIRTEEN

AN ARTICLE FIFTEEN

"War is a cowardly escape from the problems of peace."—*Thomas Mann*

5/12 Inf continued interdiction operations in AO Swordfish III.

[Intelligence Summary, 199th Inf Bde {Sep} {Lt} INTSUM 54-69]

"You are in big trouble, the man wants to bust you down to private E-zero," Top told me as soon as Tex and I got out of the truck.

Army pay grades were designated with the letter "E" followed by a number. Being a Private First Class [PFC], my pay grade was presently E-3.

I walked over to our squad bunkers to shave and get ready to see the captain.

"Military justice is to justice as military music is to music," Tony said, laughing hardily.

"What can they do to me, send me to Vietnam?" I returned.

"They could send you to LBJ," Tony replied.

LBJ was short for Long Binh jail.

The captain at his command bunker was looking angry, "Straighten your hat, PFC!" He barked at me.

I pulled my jungle hat on squarely, since it was cocked arrogantly to one side.

"Where have you been all this time you were supposed to be at Third Field?"

"At the hospital, waiting to see the dentist," I answered swallowing my sheepish grin.

"Top said he went to Third Field and your weapon was not there."

"Top made a mistake; my weapon was there the whole time."

"Dupree was hit while you were gone, don't fuck your buddy." The captain was really steamed.

"Yes sir, I heard he was going to be alright" I answered.

"Top did not find your weapon at the hospital so if you will just sign this article fifteen we've written up for you…you will only lose one pay grade for a month. Sign right here," he said holding out the papers.

"No sir, Top is wrong, I won't sign anything."

"The next step is a court martial, troop!"

"Top didn't look hard enough, I will not sign, court martial me. You'll have to take me out of the field."

The captain then dismissed me with a snarl and I never heard another word about it.

Tex told me he didn't get into any trouble, but that he was given the "R and R" to Bangkok that was due him.

"R and R" is rest and recuperation, which we were supposed to be given about every three months to catch up on our sleep and recuperate from the exhaustion. Some called it, "I and I," intercourse and intoxication.

Tex left on a jeep that day, heading for Tan Son Nhut to catch his flight to Bangkok.

I had already put in for an "R and R" to Australia, where I could do some surfing. But there was a long waiting list, so I had to wait my turn.

CHAPTER FOURTEEN

PAPPY'S AMBUSH

"War is a racket. It always has been. It is possibly the oldest, easily the most profitable, surely the most vicious."—General Smedley Butler

During reconnaissance-in-force operations 2 miles south of Duc Hoa today, an element of 5th Bn. 12th Inf discovered two enemy bodies. The enemy had been killed in action yesterday.

Two AK-47 rifles, eight magazines and three grenades were also found near the bodies." [From 199th LIB Summaries]

Six of us were air boated from FSB Kathy to our night ambush site at dusk, tired and angry. The trip flares and claymores were placed. We called in a sit rep [situation report], while eating C-rations, LRRPs and canned fruit.

"Sit-rep negative, out."

The mosquito attack had already begun, but the night passed without enemy trouble.

We were ordered to stay in place at sunup. Firing from another of our nearby ambush teams could be heard.

Pappy and his M60 machine gun team were attached to our ambush squad. The firing ebbed and flowed for about ten minutes. Then all was quiet.

Pappy climbed a tree in order to scout the area better. As he was looking around he was seen by some VC who opened up on him. Pappy was hit numerous times in the stomach and fell from the tree, dead.

David, his ammo bearer, was manning the machine gun. In a fit of rage, David stood up firing the machine gun from his hip, Rambo style. He killed two of the VC as they were trying to get away.

The remainder of the enemy squad escaped into the jungle. David recovered their AK47 rifles, one with its Chinese "pig sticker" bayonet.

A dust-off was called in to get Pappy's body. Airboats came to pick up the rest of us.

Back at Kathy the captain took the two AK47s from David but let him keep the bayonet. David also received an R and R; he was on the truck to Long Binh that afternoon.

Whenever one of us got a confirmed kill, we were given an R and R. "Body counts" were very important to our commanders, so they awarded us immediately for getting them.

Later, after David returned from R and R, he was given a bronze star award for gunning down the enemy soldiers.

All he could say was, "It don't mean nothin."

In the morning, the colonel wanted us to hump back to the ambush site where Pappy was killed. It was a long way, a mile or so and all extremely thick jungle.

Captain Williams ordered me to walk point. I had to break trail with a machete almost the entire distance. We had only air boated there in the past. It was a very hot day, we were all sweating, angry and exhausted. I could hear a lot of bitching behind me.

Early in the afternoon we finally reached the ambush site. I was quite surprised that the two dead VC soldiers were still there. Normally the enemy retrieved their dead as a soon as possible. So I was suspicious that they may be booby trapped or that we might be ambushed.

The dead enemy soldiers appeared blackened and bloated in the white hot afternoon sun. After a short look, I moved away from them because of the wretchedness of the scene.

When Tex returned from R and R he looked fatter and well rested. He was all smiles.

We were heading back to the Pineapple for another few weeks of combat patrols and ambushes. As we loaded onto the choppers, I noticed that Tex hadn't brought his rifle.

"Where's your 16, Tex?"

"I'm not taking a weapon this time; I can't see why I should." He answered.

"You've had too much R and R, my friend, are you crazy?"

Tex laughed and answered, "What reason is there to kill anyone?"

"You have a point." I said as our chopper elevated into the sky like a giant mosquito going in search of blood.

CHAPTER FIFTEEN

ANOTHER LCM RIDE AND COMBAT PATROL

"We used to wonder where war lived, what it was that made it so vile. And now we realize that we know where it lives, that it is inside ourselves."—Albert Camus

There were two combined operations in the 199th LIB's AO, one in the vicinity of An Lac Bridge, the other in Tan Nhut Triangle area. Both operations met with negative results. In the western PINEAPPLE and to the west of Vam Co Dong, interdiction operations continued.

[Intelligence Summary, 199th Inf Bde {Sep} {Lt} INTSUM 54-69]

After two more weeks of patrolling, ambushing and dusting off our casualties, we loaded onto LCMs for the ride to FSB Nancy. Per my usual, I waited for everyone else to board before I did so that I could go on last and thus be in the front, by the exit door for the dangerous ride.

Normally there were helicopter gun ships attached to us in order to suppress enemy fire from the river banks. I could hear them slapping and popping the wind in the sky above us.

One of our sergeants was already drunk. I could not understand how anyone would go into the field that way. Maybe the booze gave him nerve. I wanted to be fully awake and sober at all times.

We beached and began yet another combat patrol into the jungle.

"God I'm sick of this shit." I said as I scrambled out of the boat.

We were to sweep through another area of thick jungle. I was not walking point, so I tried to relax a little. After a few hours of hot monotony and sore, wet, feet, shots were fired at us by snipers. We all got down and no one was hurt.

To our surprise, one of the snipers actually fell out of his tree and we captured him before he could escape. Prisoners were very valuable and rare. So we headed back towards the river where the LCMs were to pick us up with our prisoner in tow.

While we struggled along another shot broke the silence of our muddy march, then angry words and shouting. The drunken sergeant had shot our prisoner in the head with his pistol for no reason other than to feed his alcoholic delusions of being a brave soldier.

I began to feel even more disgusted with this war and with the criminal behavior of some of us. For all we knew, that prisoner might have revealed information that could have saved lives, now we will never know.

The lifeless prisoner was left where he died. No one said a word to the inebriated sergeant all the way back to our pick up zone.

We rode the LCMs to FSB Nancy without further trouble. Many of us were seriously disturbed over the killing of the prisoner. We later learned that the NCO who had shot our prisoner was transferred back to Long Binh because of his drinking problem. He was out of the field and we were glad to be rid of him.

While at FSB Nancy we received a new replacement. We called them FNGs, 'fucking new guys'. He was a very tall and eighteen years old. The average age of us grunts was 19.2, during the Vietnam War.

Top ordered him to burn shit. The tall FNG looked dumbstruck and asked Tex what he was supposed to do.

Tex pointed to the outhouse and said, "Go over there and burn the shit in the officers' shitter."

The FNG said thanks and walked towards his assignment.

"He looks strong enough to carry the M60," I said.

"Ya, but he's so tall that he's libel to get his head shot off," answered Tex.

After a few minutes we could see the FNG pour diesel fuel from a jerry can over the officers' outhouse and then ignite it with his Zippo lighter.

It exploded in a huge ball of flames in the oppressive heat of the day. The tall FNG stood their watching, looking somewhat pleased with his handiwork.

Top came running over cussing like a sailor. Tex and I could not stop laughing.

The Colonel sent the tall FNG back to Long Binh that afternoon.

We never saw him again. I figured that he had found a unique way to get out of the field, regardless of whether he knew it or not.

CHAPTER SIXTEEN

BATTLE FATIGUE

"A great war leaves the country with three armies - an army of cripples, an army of mourners, and an army of thieves."—German Proverb

I was exhausted and having trouble getting any rest or sleep so I went to see our company doctor.

Captain Barnes, our doctor, listened to my complaints about being dead tired, feeling dizzy a lot and that I could not seem to think very well. I told him that I was too exhausted to be effective in the field.

Captain Barnes gave me a small pill called "Valium," told me to take it with water and get some sleep.

First thing next morning I was back at the doctor's hooch.

"That pill didn't work, I still feel totally exhausted, even worse than yesterday, Doc."

Doc Barnes thought a bit then told me to get on the first vehicle heading for Redcatcher brigade main base at Long Binh as he wrote me a prescription for bed rest due to combat fatigue.

The folks at brigade were supposed to see that I got four days of rest and sleep so that I could get back into the field as soon as possible.

After I removed my boots and settled into a bunk, I was ordered to get my rifle and ammo and report to the perimeter for guard duty because the base was on very high alert. All infantrymen to the perimeter was the order of the day.

That evening after chow, I settled back into my bunk for some sleep. I was just dozing off when I heard the high pitch whistle of incoming rockets.

Everyone was running to get to the safety of sandbagged bunkers. I got back into my boots as fast as possible, grabbed my rifle and a bandolier of ammo and joined them in the bunkers until ordered back out to the perimeter again for the long night.

Still no rest for the weary.

Next morning, I was ordered to report to a captain so that he could give me some high security trash to burn, it seems they just did not have enough grunts around for all of the work that needed to be done.

This trash was so important that they had a special place, which was enclosed by a high chain link fence and a locked gate. Inside was a small revolving wire cage in which the top security papers were placed and burned while I turned the crank that rotated the cage to insure that everything was consumed in the fire.

This went on for two more days with only minor variations. I was given various chores to do during the day and we got rocketed every night. I was not getting any sleep or rest.

I asked the medical officer in charge to send me back to the field so that I could get some rest.

He laughed while writing out the paperwork.

"Sorry, PFC Seidenberg, we can't order Charlie to stop his attacks.

CHAPTER SEVENTEEN

AGENT ORANGE

"No country is so wild and difficult but men will make it a theater of war."—Ambrose Bierce

Elements of 5th Bn. 12th Inf. found the body of one Viet Cong killed earlier by artillery fire from Delta Btry, 2nd Bn. 40th Arty. The infantrymen also destroyed two sampans and located a small enemy medical cache in an area 3 miles northwest of Ben Luc.

[From 199th LIB Summaries]

Back at FSB Kathy, nothing had changed.

We were heading into the Pineapple again for another two or three weeks of combat patrols, ambushes, mosquitoes, wet feet, LRRPs and other assorted miseries.

This time we were to begin at night, in darkness. I was selected to walk point.

I laughed when I saw Tex carrying a ninety millimeter recoilless rifle, which fired rounds that were about the size of a football. It was the largest weapon in our light infantry arsenal, weighing about thirty five pounds. The antipersonnel [canister], rounds Tex carried for it weighed nearly seven pounds each.

I guessed he had already changed his mind about killing folks.

The first leg of this mission was on the LCMs.

Once the sun set, we boarded, the diesel motors revved and off we noisily sailed, up the brown, lazy river.

Upon beaching and after we established our formation, I led the patrol single file and at proper intervals into the moonless night. The mud was ankle deep so I wasn't worried about buried booby traps, but being ambushed did weigh on me.

I walked heel to toe, very slowly and quietly, not wanting to make any noise. I couldn't help making that sucking sound with every step, as my boots disengaged the sticky mud.

It was very hard going, one frightening step at a time, straining to make sense of what little I could see until we finally came to another river.

Word was passed that this was to be our night blocking force site and of course there wasn't much dry ground to camp upon.

My feet were soaked and I was dead tired, so I kept my boots on all night. I had to pull two hours of guard duty anyhow.

In the morning we loaded back into the LCMs for a defoliant spraying mission.

Two of us were to spray the defoliant, called "Agent Orange" [dioxin being one of its active ingredients], from a large sprayer onto the lush, brilliant green foliage that grew prolifically along the banks. This was done to deny the enemy cover from which to ambush us while we were traveling on the river.

The rest of us simply guarded or sat around talking, eating and or resting.

The defoliant operation went on all day. We met some sampans on the river and had to check them to make sure they weren't carrying enemies or their supplies.

One small sampan wasn't responding to our signals so the lieutenant ordered me to fire at them. I didn't want to hit anyone with a bullet so I found a flare gun and shot one over their sampan. That got their attention and they pulled over so that we could see what they were hauling.

I was proud of the way that I had interpreted and executed the lieutenant's order because no one was hurt and the sampan in question was innocently hauling a load of tiny fish.

The folks in the sampan waved and smiled at us as they continued on their way downriver.

CHAPTER EIGHTEEN

"THERE IS A LAST TIME FOR EVERYTHING" – THE OLD GRINGO

5/12 Inf continued interdiction operations in AO Swordfish III

LCM to 3 B report getting hit with 3 RPG rounds from south bank reports a lot of causlties Razor Back on station putting stricks in area now.

S-3 told S-3 air told to get down to the other LCM8 S-3 air said the fire came from 644904.

LCM8 [63B] said he has a total of a personnel 1 litter and 5 ambulatory.

Requested dust from Saigon dust off. Gave as dust off 43 ETA 15 minutes.

D Co told Bn that he has 1 KIA 2 litter 5 ambulatory Razor Back 40 [LFT] dusted off D Co's most wounded which leaves a total 1 LCM closed Claudette with D Co aboard. LFT released.

DO informed 1099th Boat Co of contact involving their LCM 17.

Bde with usually reliable agent report 2043 vic xs 642908 C-3 [Bde requests 5/12 put arty into that location.

D Co said he request not to send his TA's out tonight due to the darkness the fatigue and possible booby traps. S-3 air told him he can cut one of his TA's but the one to the northwest must go out. [From 199th LIB Summaries]

Spot Reports from Bde—#1 02 March C 5/12 found at 067025 15 60mm rnds with fuses. 16 RPG rnds, one 82mm bipod,

50 AK 50 rnds, 50 50caliber rnds, 6 entrenching tools #2)2 March C 5/12 found at XT 065025 1 bicycle pump, 200 feet of nylon rope, two 82mm rnds with fuses, 1 pistol belt, 1 VC body 4 days old, #3 02 March C 5/12 found at XT 063125 1 AK 47, 4 AK magazines, 1 RPG, 2 canteens, 1 pistol belt, 2 VC bodies 2-3 days old KIA'd by air.

DO told D Co CO to get with his people and set a complete resummary of what took place in today's contact to include the names of his personnel that was wounded and dusted off. D Co CO asked if he wanted this tonight, D.C. answered on the affirmative.

D CO gave a summary of this afternoons contact. At Appnex 021705 LCM was hit by 2 RPG rnds, at the same time the 1st went over the boat.

The second hit the boat but didn't explode. The third hit to the front of the LCM Killing Garcia. Two more didn't go off, seem to be set to hit boat at certain pts. on the side of canal. Received AK automatic fire from estimated 3 personnel. Boat and LFT immediately returned fire. Observed 2-3 personnel running north LCM proceeded down the canal, beached, called dust off. Later sweep of contacted area revealed several trails leading north. Also found 1 piece of Chinese Communist C-4.

Bde D.C. indicated that the Bde CG wants to see the planned routes for patrols out of Claudette into the contact area to be conducted on 03 March.

D.C. gave Bde a radar sighting out of Cathy. 2242 06 personnel vic XS 638869 Grid was given to arty. 81mm shot 2250 105's shot 2253.

LCM8 [63B] told S-3 air that his higher has put an administrative dead line on him and LCM8 [63B] for reasons really unknown. But one LCM8 was under attack today with out a LFT as cover. [From 5/12 199 LIB Daily Staff Journal, 2 March 1969]

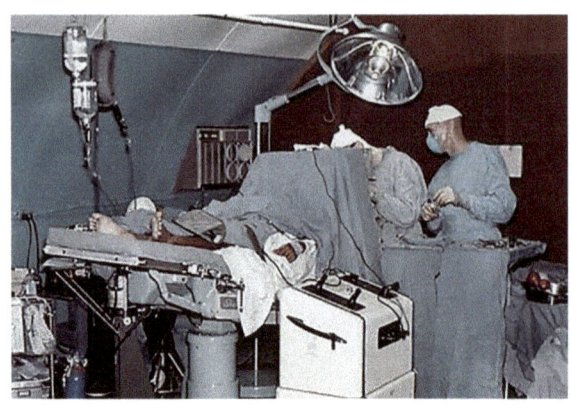

Everything went inexorably black, a venue of complete nothingness which I had never experienced before; a lifeless void.

Am I finally asleep?

Opening my eyes, all I could see was an amazing whiteness. So terribly white that it sparkled and shimmered. The whiteness was alien, blinding and painful. I was dizzy, confused and totally forgetful.

Now I had absolutely no memory of anything that had occurred in my entire life.

I have died and now I'm on this white cloud traveling to heaven, I thought to myself.

An angel was asking me if I knew what had happened.

"I think I was in a war?"

She smiled and said, "Yes, you were injured but you'll be OK soon."

Then I noticed that the blinding whiteness was simply a sheet on the bed I was in. I hadn't seen anything this white in a very long time.

Another wave of black nothingness washed over me, taking me under again. Blackness and nothingness had returned for how long, I don't know.

Sometime later, I was able to see again.

An artillery piece was firing away from the inside of my head, shooting round after round, trying to blow another hole in my skull.

I felt something strange on my forehead; a long line of stitches ran from above my right ear, along the top of my forehead and all the way to the other side, under my scalp. There were tiny chunks of metal scattered about, slightly poking through the skin on the right side of my head, face and neck.

A new depression, about the size of a fifty cent piece, resided just above and forward of my right ear. Plastic tubes ran from both of my wrists. Another tube came out of the tip of my penis. I noticed it when I tried to urinate, which seemed to take hours to complete.

A dense pattern of red cobwebs inhabited my right eye, making it nearly impossible to see through them. My ears were ringing, on and on and on.

I was in the black water again, another huge wave crashing on me, going under, floating, twisting, turning round and round, then sinking down, down, down, into oblivion.

Tony, Tex and Doc Wayne, our medic, visited me in the field hospital. They said we were ambushed with RPGs [rocket propelled grenades], while being transported on an LCM [landing craft, medium].

The VC fired RPGs into our boat. David was blown in half; he was standing right beside me.

My rifle was hit by some flying fragments and began to "cook off." The bullets were exploding from the heat, so Tony threw it overboard. He said that the captain tried to charge him replacement cost for tossing it!

The boat was sinking; "We were knee deep in blood by the time we got it over to the bank. Those of us still able assaulted into the jungle, but didn't find anything," Tony said.

"Command hung us out to dry on the Vam Co Dong River; we had no air cover, none, goddamn REMFS" [rear echelon mother fuckers], Tex added.

It was standard operating procedure for each LCM to be covered by a helicopter gunship to suppress enemy fire from the river banks.

After restarting my heart, Doc Wayne sat me up out of the muddy, bloody water. Doc was frantically trying to stop the blood gushing from the side of my head. The dust off chopper was on its way to our position.

Doc rode on the chopper with me back to the field surgery hospital and could not get the combat knife out of my head. I kept trying to knife him every time I became semiconscious. He told me he had to restart my heart twice more.

Doc Wayne also said that I was the only one that he was able to save from our company who was severely wounded.

WESTERN UNION

Telegram

MRS SUE SEIDENBERG

PDB=FAX WASHINGTON DC VIA ANAHEIM CALIF 4=

DON'T PHONE REPORT DELIVERY=

1969 MAR 5 AM 7 20

THE SECRETARY OF THE ARMY HAS ASKED ME TO EXPRESS HIS DEEP REGRET THAT YOUR SON PRIVATE FIRST CLASS DANIEL SEIDENBERG JR WAS PLACED ON THE VERY SERIOUSLY ILL LIST IN VIETNAM ON 2 MARCH 1969 AS THE RESULT OF A PENETRATING FRAGMENT WOUND TO THE RIGHT

TEMPLE HE WAS ON A MILITARY MISSION WHEN ENGAGED A HOSTILE FORCE IN FIREFIGHT HE WAS HOSPITALIZED IN VIETNAM ADDRESS MAIL TO HIM AT THE HOSPITAL MAIL SECTION APO SF 96381 IN THE JUDGEMENT OF THE ATTENDING PHYSICIAN HIS CONDITION IS OF SUCH SEVERITY THAT THERE IS CAUSE FOR CONCERN PLEASE BE ASSURED THAT THE BEST MEDICAL FACILITIES AND DOCTORS

HAVE BEEN MADE AVAILABLE AND EVERY MEASURE IS BEING TAKEN TO AID HIM YOU WILL BE KEPT

INFORMED OF ANY SIGNIFICANT CHANGES IN HIS CONDIDTION=

KENNETH G WICKHAM MAJOR GENERAL

USA C379 THE ADJUTANT GENERAL=

My hometown newspaper published a false story about the ambush which was provided to them by the army, "Son of Lompoc Wounded in Action."

The U.S. Department of Defense said Wednesday PFC Daniel Seidenberg, Junior, 21; son of Daniel and Mrs. Seidenberg has been critically wounded and is hospitalized in Vietnam.

The communication to the parents said that Seidenberg suffered a wound in the right temple while in action as advance man on an American patrol probing deep into Communist territory near Bien Hoa in search of arms caches. He was caught in a fire fight. The authorities said that he was too critically wounded to be flown out of Vietnam to hospitals in Japan or America. He had been in Vietnam for three months.

When I read this news story, after arriving back in the states, I became very angry because it seemed that command was trying to blame me for walking us into an enemy ambush.

CHAPTER NINETEEN

TOKYO SNOW

"During times of universal deceit, telling the truth becomes a revolutionary act."—George Orwell

SY WA414 XV GOVT PD=WASHINGTON DC 10 331P EST

1969 MAR 9 PM 4 35

MRS SUE SEIDENBERG

DON'T PHONE CHECK DLY CHGS

I AM PLEASED TO INFORM YOU THAT YOUR SON PRIVATE FIRST CLASS DANIEL SEIDENBERG JR HAS BEEN REMOVED FROM THE VERY SERIOUSLY ILL LIST. HE IS ABLE TO COMMUICATE EVACUATION TO THE UNTIED STATES IS CONTEMPLATED IN APPROXIMATELY TWO WEEKS.= SINCE HIS CONDITION IS NO LONGER CONSIDERED SERIOUS NO FURTHER REPORTS WILL BE FURNISHED. I SHARE YOUR HOPE

THAT HE WILL HAVE A RAPID RECOVERY= KG WICKHAM MAJ GENL USA C-1716 THE ADJUTANT GENL.

A week or so later I was transferred to Camp Drake, in Japan. I was able to get into a wheelchair and go outside where there was about a foot of snow covering everything; more blinding whiteness.

I was overwhelmed with survivor's euphoria, being alive never felt like this before. A near death experience can certainly elevate one's morale in spite of the pain marching double time inside of my brain.

When I wheeled into the bathroom and looked into the mirror, I was shocked by my reflection which was that of an old man with a scarred, shaved head and a swollen, black and blue face.

I was very happy to see modern plumbing after so long without it. Sinks, toilets and yet more whiteness, it was stunning, almost surreal in its gleaming cleanliness. I spent what seemed like hours just sitting on that amazing throne.

The starched, white uniformed army nurse was filling a large syringe with antibiotic and checking her ward list.

Because I had incurred an infection from my wounds, I required four injections of antibiotics per day.

She walked over to the bed where her first patient to be injected should have been, then she realized that this was the one who had wheeled into the bathroom as she came on duty.

Walking to the door of the bathroom, she called my name softly so as not to awaken the others.

"OK, be right out," I answered.

"Come on, it's for your own good," she replied.

I slid off the magnificent plumbing and into my wheelchair, and then rolled back to my bed.

Looking around for the nurse but only seeing the other wounded guys I was again overwhelmed by massive feelings of gratitude for being alive and seemingly being better off than the others on the ward.

I climbed back into bed, lay down and tried to ignore the pounding artillery barrage being fired inside of my head. My ears were still ringing incessantly.

No pain medicine could be given to those with severe head wounds.

Suddenly the nurse was standing by me. She motioned for me to roll onto my side. I pulled my pajamas down enough for her to stick the needle into to my buttock. When she pushed the plunger, painful tentacles began spreading just under my skin, like fire lazily igniting in a hay loft.

I said, "Thanks," as she moved away from me and onto the next injection three or four beds down the row.

The next morning, a youngish nurse was tasked to get me cleaned up. My ears were incrusted with all manner of debris and Vietnamese dirt.

She worked away for what seemed like hours even using a small suction device normally used to clean out a baby's nostrils.

I heard her say softly, "My god don't you ever bathe?"

I didn't say anything but thought to myself, we didn't have bathrooms in the field, no showers, and no tubs...not even any clean water, sorry about that.

Cleanliness was pretty low on our list of worries in the field.

The pain was pulsating and increasing as another artillery barrage began inside my brain. I drifted back under that huge, black wave again. Sleep was the only way to escape the painful barrages.

I was back in the field, somehow. A night ambush was just getting underway. Hand grenades were being exchanged. I was taking them from my web gear and from a stack I had on my poncho liner. I threw fastballs, high hard ones which arched into the dark night.

An incoming grenade landed right next to me with a sullen thud. I grabbed for it but it slipped from my shaking hand. I grabbed it again and lifted it for a return throw. It exploded in my face.

I was sweating and in even more pain when I finally awoke from this nightmare. The fear had returned to my newly found world of whiteness.

Later that afternoon I received a phone call from Ted, one of my best friends back home. When I heard his voice, I recognized it but could not remember his name. My brain still wasn't working very well.

I had forgotten nearly everything; my past seemed inexplicably distant and unknowable. Slowly, eventually, after many years, most of it came back to me, other than about two or three weeks preceding my injury.

After a few weeks recuperating in Japan I was finally going back to the states on a massive hospital aircraft. It was huge, with row upon row of cots, stacked floor to ceiling with the wounded.

I was still getting the painful injections every six hours.

We landed in Oakland, California and I was transferred to another airlift heading for Brooke Army Medical Center, Fort Sam Houston in San Antonio, Texas.

CHAPTER TWENTY

THE NEUROLOGY WARD

"You know, once on the tiger's back, we can't pick the time to dismount."—George Ball

Trays of food were being wheeled around to the thirty or so head wounded soldiers when I was told that I could walk to the cafeteria, since I was now able to do so.

"It's just down that hall past the burn ward and then to your left, down the stairway." The nurse told me.

As I slowly shuffled through the burn ward in my army PJs and robe, I became thankful that I was not a patient on that ward. The soldiers there were not recognizable. Their faces were now featureless. Some of them were suspended in weird contraptions that looked like torture racks from some long gone grisly era. I decided to stop looking at them to maintain any appetite.

When I started down the stairway I almost stumbled, it had been a very long time since I had been on stairs and everything looked flat seeing with just one eye. So I slowed down even more, held on to the rail and felt the stairs with my feet as I descended.

I picked up a tray and filled it with chow. It felt good to eat regular food, even army food and sit at a real table in a real chair!

Next day, the nurse gave me luggage duty. I was to report to the baggage room in the basement to help them haul things around.

When I arrived there, I was so dizzy and in so much pain that I immediately went back to my bunk on the ward to rest. Later, the nurse saw me; I told her I was not yet ready to do any work.

She was not happy with me and angrily told me that she would try to get me off of her ward as soon as possible.

"And cut that mustache off, try to look like a real soldier!" She attempted to order me like a stern drill sergeant.

I rolled over, placing my good ear against the pillow so as not to hear her anymore.

Sunday was visiting day, many parents and other relatives would be arriving in just a few minutes. The nurse came in and turned on every television set. There was one for every few beds, hanging from the walls like one eyed monsters.

When she turned on the one nearest me; "ring around the collar" echoed through my throbbing brain.

"We don't want to watch that garbage."

The nurse answered, "It's not for you; it's for the visitors."

I noticed during visiting hours that I was the only patient on the ward that could still talk. I saw tears running down the cheeks of some of the other wounded soldiers.

One night there was a loud thunderstorm which transported many of us back into the combat zone....the flashes of lightning and the sonic explosions were all too similar to the hell we had gone through so recently.

About a week went by before the head nurse had me transferred to the medical hold over barracks. I was glad to be off the neurology ward and not to have to walk through the burn ward three times a day.

Days later the Captain of the medical holdover barracks summoned me to his office and awarded me the Purple Heart medal without ceremony or even a handshake, not even a thank you for your service.

I was not offended considering what I had gone through since joining the army.

A lawyer from the adjutant's office visited to advise me regarding leaving the active army. He said I would be placed on the temporary disability retired list with an eighty percent disability for now. My condition would be reviewed later to determine whether I would be reactivated or placed on the permanent retired list.

He then said; "When you get back on the block, go to the Social Security Administration and apply for disability insurance and do not take "no" for an answer!"

"Yes sir."

Next day the neurologist gave me some further advice.

"You've incurred a wound for which the survival rate in Vietnam is just .02 percent and 98 percent of the survivors are now vegetables. I'm giving you this prescription for "Dilantin," an anti-seizure medication. However, my advice for you is to smoke pot since it is much more forgiving for your condition. I know it's illegal, so be careful!"

This all occurred in early summer, 1969. I was excited and happy to be leaving the army, regardless of the medical constraints that I was just beginning to learn to live with.

The worry of being recalled to active duty took up residency in the back of my brain, though.

CHAPTER TWENTY-ONE

BACK IN THE WORLD

"There is always hope, but not for us."—Franz Kafka

I was still having severe headaches that would last three or four days at a time. I would become extremely dizzy every time I looked directly upwards or stood up too quickly. My ears were ringing like church bells on Easter Sunday and I could see clearly from only one eye but I was elated to be out of the hospital, away from the army and combat duty.

My steadfast friend, Ted, invited me to stay at his house in Seattle. So I unpacked my few belongings and moved into his attic.

Ted had moved from Tukwila to Seattle while I was in Vietnam in order to attend the University of Washington. He had saved enough money to quit his job at Boeing aircraft and go to school full time.

Attending college, forgetting about the war and constructing a future were my goals now.

The Veterans Administration awarded me a hundred percent disability and their counselor advised me to apply for vocational rehabilitation because my army work and training did not apply to civilian employment.

I took entrance tests and signed up for classes at the University of Washington. Because I was on academic probation from Santa Barbara City College, I had to take even more tests to get into UW.

As I was walking to classes one day, a passing car backfired. I instantly and instinctively hit the ground and scrambled under a parked car for protection. Some other students saw this and began to point and laugh.

I waited for them to leave before crawling from under the parked car. My reaction to the backfire had shocked and surprised me a lot more than it had amused the other students.

My right eye seemed to be healing and I could see better through the few remaining red "cobwebs." The VA ophthalmologist told me to see him if I noticed any changes in my vision so that is what I did. I made an appointment but had to wait three months for it.

"You'll need surgery to repair the retinal detachment, and why didn't you get in here sooner?" the doctor implored.

"I wanted to, I came in as soon as I noticed the change but I had to wait in line, Doc."

Scar tissue formed by the healing of the traumatic hemorrhage inside my eye had torn the retina and optical fluid was pushing under it; this would lead to blindness if left untreated.

Subsequently I had three very painful surgeries on my right eye, in the space of a year or so to repair the retina and relieve post operative glaucoma, but the eye could not be saved.

The almost constant, severe, post operative pain in my right eye caused the headaches to worsen so I began to take codeine tablets. I was taking Dilantin for seizure control also at this time. Getting out of bed was becoming very difficult. I felt heavy, like I was severely drugged.

The war in Vietnam was raging on; my brigade was tasked to join the incursion into Cambodia. I felt sorry for the grunts still there… being wounded and killed every day for no apparent reason.

I seemed to be going crazy over that and the way our government was using them, plus the severe pain I was in nearly every day.

I decided to seek help from the Veterans Administration mental health clinic.

"Doc, I can't go to sleep. I can't stay asleep. I'm jumpy. I can't tolerate crowds. I'm tired all of the time. I can barely relate to other people or to what I once thought were my own goals. I can't stand the noise. I can't stand the quiet. My head, neck and face hurt most of the time. I need to talk about the war."

"We don't talk about that here," the V.A. psychiatrist abruptly ordered.

"Let us talk about your childhood, Mom and Dad. How's your sex life…tell me?"

The doctor rocked back in his large chair and looked out of the window.

"I'm going to have to medicate this patient, he presents symptoms of paranoia," he thought to himself.

"But, Doc, I'm very bothered by some of the stuff that happened to me in the army, putting aside practically getting my head blown away followed by all of the surgeries."

"I fully understand, however, I must ask you not to speak of that now…I want to hear about your sex life."

"I just got out of the hospital, before that I just got out of the jungle…I have no sex life. I can't talk about something that doesn't exist."

"Alright then, what about your mother and father?"

"Forget it, Doc."

The doctor began to busy himself completing his clinic notes; I could read upside down "paranoid schizophrenic" as he wrote it.

Next, he wrote a prescription for "Thorazine" and handed it to me saying; "I want to see you next month, same time, same place. Please take all of the medication on schedule, according to the instructions that are on the container and we'll see how you are feeling at that time."

I left his office and headed to the pharmacy to get the prescription filled.

Walking to and from classes at the University of Washington, a fellow student asked me what happened to my eye. I was wearing a black patch because the bright light bothered me.

"I was injured in Vietnam."

"You deserved it," he said as he turned and walked away.

I took some of the pills prescribed by the VA psychiatrist but they made me feel even worse. I was having trouble getting out of bed; it felt like I was struggling under a ton of wet cement. Walking or even thinking was a huge chore.

"I will never take any more pills prescribed by the VA," I thought to myself as I flushed the rest of the bottle down the toilet.

CHAPTER TWENTY-TWO

DAYS OF RAGE

"When the power of love overcomes the love of power the world will know peace."—Jimi Hendrix

I continued attending classes at the University of Washington, studied hard and read a lot.

I was unsure that my brain worked as well as it used to, so I decided to take up something different that would require entirely new thinking as a further test.

Steve, a fellow student, gave me a small book "Chess the Easy Way," by Rueben Fine. It was something new, much like learning a foreign language. I took up the game and began playing here and there. I found it to be bloodless combat without physical hostilities but giving me a bit of that addictive combat adrenalin rush while testing my brain power.

Steve asked me to join him downtown for a Vietnam War protest, the protesters, mostly college students and others of draft age were going to shut down the city. The slogan of the day was, "no more business as usual."

We were going to be a squad, Steve, Bill, Wally and I. We wore red armbands so as to be able to easily identify one another within the huge crowds.

The University was already closed by the protesting students. There were burning trash dumpsters blockading every entrance, police were chasing and beating some of the protesting students on campus, so no classes were being held.

Thousands of us walked from the University district all the way to downtown Seattle. There were a lot of non students, average working folks with small children. Some were old enough to be grandparents, joining the protest along the route. It seemed that finally most Americans were fed up with our bloody war on Vietnam.

Along the route, pickup trucks with men wearing hard hats inside drove slowly by spitting at us. I wore an army jungle hat and fatigue shirt with my Purple Heart medal pinned on. I was spit at a few times and called a communist.

Every so often along the route, some of the men in hard hats would stop, pile out of their trucks brandishing axe handles and hit unfortunate protesters that could not get out of the way fast enough.

This was nearly like being in combat, so I felt somewhat comfortable but grimly familiar with the action.

Once we arrived downtown, the streets were alive, undulating, overflowing with folks. The noise from the crowd was deafening.

Any business that had not already closed and locked its doors was entered and "trashed." That is, protesters would run inside and dump their trash cans, chairs, anything we could find onto the floor and implore them to close for the day. "No more business as usual!"

Business people on second floors and above threw things at the protesters or simply watched it all unfold.

The jam packed streets echoed with the shouts of: "No more war... Hell no, we won't go...No more business as usual!" as the marchers continued their protest well into the day.

Battalions of buses arrived with police in full riot gear, wearing helmets, carrying shields, night sticks and tear gas canisters as well as the usual pistols and shotguns.

The police attempted to divide the protesting crowds into smaller, more manageable groups and chase the smaller, splintered groups into blind alleys, beat them and or arrest some of them.

Most of us noted this tactic and avoided being caught in the police traps.

Agent provocateurs tried to harangue the marching, chanting crowds to do violent actions, calling them "pussies," "wimps," "queers" and worse, but no one took them seriously and many of us shouted them down and told them to stop trying to incite violence.

Towards the end of the afternoon, the student leaders gathered to decide what to do next. They agreed to march back to the university district by the same route that they had come. Many of us disagreed and advised them not to take that route, for they had to cross a very long bridge that was part of the Seattle freeway system. I knew that bridge would be a perfect place for the police to trap and ambush them with tear gas.

So my squad took the long route home, we walked under the bridge, using only the surface streets. Soon as we arrived back at the house, we turned on the television and watched the main body of the protest being tear gassed on the bridge. Many of them panicked and ran through police blockades, jumped down the off ramps breaking legs and incurring other injuries.

Classes at the university finally resumed after another week of protests. I had taken a full class load for the first time that spring quarter, so I was studying almost constantly.

CHAPTER TWENTY-THREE

AT WAR WITH THE VETERANS ADMINISTRATION,

THE POLICE AND MYSELF

"To care for him who shall have borne the battle and for his widow, and his orphan"—The U.S. Department of Veterans Affairs Motto

In June, when spring quarter ended, I received a letter from the Veterans Administration that stated, "Since full time schooling is equivalent to full time employment, you are no longer considered disabled under the law."

The VA cut my disability compensation money in half, from four hundred dollars a month; subtracted another two hundred dollars for school expenses, so now I was getting about two hundred dollars a month.

I could no longer afford to attend school at the University of Washington. I scheduled an appointment with the V.A. rehabilitation counselor to find out why my six year program for a master's degree was terminated.

"Sorry, the law is the law," was his pat answer.

I had also applied for Social Security disability insurance as advised by the army lawyer.

Ted had won a scholarship to Princeton University for a PhD program in anthropology and was busily preparing to move to New Jersey.

I packed my old Ford van with all of my belongings and drove back to Santa Barbara. I wanted to get back into the surf, if possible, which I had missed so dearly.

Santa Barbara seemed to have not changed much since I left. Here was the warm sunshine, the soft breezes and the cool green-blue waves breaking on the tan speckled sands that had been washed by last winter's tides and swells.

I found some good pals from high school; we all pitched in and rented a house that was condemned. It was all that we could afford. The house had many rooms and was right beside the 101 freeway, just a block from the railroad tracks. The nearly constant noise from both made sleeping very nearly impossible. I was still having severe headaches, dizziness and nightmares of combat every few days.

One night, while asleep, a loud explosion coming from the freeway accosted my slumber. I was still in Vietnam and we were coming under a ground assault at fire support base Nancy. Rocket propelled grenades and small arms fire was peppering the place like a violent storm straight from hell. The Vietcong were now inside of our wire and running around shooting everyone they found. We were being overrun.

I was running hard when I came to our lookout tower; I began to climb it, having nowhere else to go but up. A Vietcong soldier was right on my heels and trying to grab one of my feet. As we approached the top of the tower, it started to fall over. I held on tightly as it fell completely throwing me into the jungle outside of our perimeter.

Miraculously, I was unhurt. I quickly got to my feet and took off through the jungle trying to outrun the Vietcong still chasing after me.

Finding a good hiding spot under some logs and bushes, I slid right in. The Vietcong were still searching for me, joking with one another and poking their long bayonets into the brush every so often.

Suddenly one of them was standing directly above my hiding spot, as he was about to stick his bayonet into my chest, I awoke, sweating and shaking, my brain ambushed by yet another nightmare of Vietnam.

I made an appointment to see the Santa Barbara county veterans' service officer to get advice about VA compensation payments. After relating my army record and recent history with the VA, Ernie told me that I should appeal their decision.

We set to work writing my appeal and after about a year of waiting the appeals board finally decided in my favor. I was paid back the money they had taken away and I was once again awarded 100% disability.

As the war on Vietnam continued it seemed to be a permanent part of our lives; the rage against it had also engulfed Santa Barbara.

Isla Vista is a tiny college community ten miles west of Santa Barbara. It is well known for its parties, beaches and fast life-style.

With 1,000 students and street people shouting "Burn, baby, burn!" youths set fire to piles of debris and shoved them through the Bank of America doorway. Some of the students argued that the attack was senseless. The burners, unable to articulate their reasons, answered that the bank was a "symbol of corporate corruption." Time Magazine, March 9, 1970

June 4th, [1970], the people of Isla Vista again attempted to burn the bank, battling the police in the streets. When the fighting ceased, 667 people had been arrested. Incomplete figures showed numerous instances of police brutality, including: 92 cases of unprovoked beatings, 43 cases of illegal entry, 26 cases of willful destruction of property, 6 cases of threats of death accompanied by the use of weapons, and 5 sexual offenses against women. Islavista.org

President Nixon had widened the war to include Cambodia and was conducting a third drive into that countries' border region with Vietnam.

I drove the van out to Isla Vista the day of the last attempt to burn the Bank of America......angry, frustrated and awash in psychic pain, to vent and watch the protest.

Hundreds of students were there milling about, some of them planning to burn the bank and battle the police who were arriving by the carload.

There must have been perhaps twenty police cars that formed in single file and began circling the bank like early American settlers circling their wagons for defense against marauding Indians.

Many in the crowd began to throw rocks, bricks, bottles....anything they could find at the police cars that were slowly circling continuously around the bank.

Students and other protesters could not approach the bank due to the tight cordon of police cars, it was a stalemate. A steady barrage of thrown objects continued, unabated. Day slowly faded to night. The student leaders of the crowd huddled and decided on a diversionary tactic to draw the rotating wall of police cars away from the bank.

"To the rot see building, burn it!"

Many of the students began walking towards the UCSB campus where the old wooden barracks style ROTC, [Reserve Officers' Training Corps], building stood...dry, vulnerable and unguarded.

Exactly as the students had planned, the police stopped their circling and began driving over to the university campus to meet the new student juggernaut.

After about half the angry crowd had left for the campus, the police cars were all gone, not one of them stayed to protect the bank.

A few members of the remaining crowd rolled a full trash dumpster onto the sidewalk in front of the bank and set it afire. Then it was shoved, flaming and sparking, into the double glass doors of the Bank of America. The crowd roared their approval in the dark, crazy night. Smoke and flames entered the bank through the crunching, flying, broken glass of the doors.

The crowd went wild, their yelling became even louder as smoke began filling the bank.

Suddenly the crowd became silent. The bank, after the last riotous burning, had been rebuilt bunker style, with a ceiling sprinkler system that now activated, almost instantly extinguishing the bright flames. Only thick, grey-white smoke was now billowing from the dumpster and out through the shattered doors.

The crowd booed, hissed and grumbled their displeasure; the bank would not burn, not on this night.

Back in the war again; we were in an ambush, rifle fire coming and going. Fog and smoke of war so thick that I seemed to be lost between the lines of fire, I forgot what side I was fighting for. Did it matter?

As I was loading another magazine into my rifle I heard a soft voice say above me, "I'm leaving now."

Rolling over onto my back, looking up, I saw my soul wistfully floating away.

"Where are you going?"

"I'm leaving, you're a murderer."

"No, that's wrong; I'm simply trying to survive all of this!"

"Goodbye."

My spirit was abandoning me, but it was only another nightmare.

CHAPTER TWENTY-FOUR

SOCIAL SECURITY DISABILITY INSURANCE

"Only our concept of time makes it possible for us to speak of the Day of Judgment by that name: in reality it is a summary court in perpetual session."—Franz Kafka

While I was still attending the University of Washington, on the Veterans Administration vocational rehabilitation program, I remembered and followed the good advice given me by the Army lawyer when I was given leave from Brooke Army hospital, Fort Sam Houston at San Antonio, Texas. After filling out the claim forms and attaching copies of my service medical records, I began the long wait for a reply.

About six months later the reply came from the Social Security administration; "You are not considered disabled under the law."

I began my appeal, stating that I disagreed with the decision and requested a court hearing.

Another year went by before I finally received a date for the federal court hearing which thankfully would be held in Santa Barbara so I would not have to travel far.

No doctors were called to testify as to my disabilities, symptoms or prognosis. I was asked only if I could still drive a car, to which I answered yes.

The hearing did not take very long, about half an hour. The federal law judge called only one witness, a man who was supposed to be an employment expert. He testified that considering my work record, age and intellect; I could work in a factory or park cars.

I was unable to reconcile the fact that I was considered 80% disabled by the army and 100% disabled by the VA, but not disabled at all according to the Social Security Administration.

They were trying to discourage me with a view to making me give up my claim and thus saving money and furthering their own government careers.

I would drive over to the beach at sunrise and check for good waves every morning I was able. When the waves were large enough to surf, I would hall out my board and ride for an hour or so until other surfers would show up. I didn't like crowds, so I would exit the water as the others began paddling out.

Too often I would pay for my surfing with another severe headache; the cold water and hot sun did it, I figured.

By the winter of 1975, my friend Ted was living and working in New York City. He was scheduled to do some research in Spain and asked me if I wanted to housesit his apartment on the West Side very near Central Park.

Of course I accepted and was anxious to play chess with the professionals in the Big Apple. I looked at this as a chance to cram chess strategy and tactics over the board any time, night and day.

Bobby Fischer, a New Yorker, was at this time world champion so chess had become very popular, more popular than ever here in the USA.

Most of the best chess action was at night so I began sleeping in the daytime and awakening at dusk to play with the masters and chess hustlers all night long; walking back to the apartment at sunrise.

Our war on Vietnam was still raging, I didn't want to think about it or have anything to do with it anymore and this seemed to be the mode that most Americans were in by 1975. It was enough that I had to deal with the loss of vision, severe three day headaches, overwhelming fatigue, post traumatic stress and temporal lobe seizures.

I played through February, March and April, living on Asian food and pizza off the New York streets.

I felt right at home, the ladies seemed to like me, inviting me to their apartments, out for a drink and to other activities but it took me about two weeks to learn the language…the New Yorkers speak very, very fast!

I was walking home from the Chess House, early one morning near the end of April when I saw the headline on the New York Times; "VIETNAM WAR ENDS!"

An overwhelming sense of joy and happiness caused me to shout: "The war is finally over!"

Others, out that morning, looked at me like I was just another crazy among the many on the New York streets.

One person replied, "So what?"

Others did not share my emotions that morning. No one other than me seemed to care to even note the end of our ten year struggle which had killed tens of thousands of my fellow soldiers as well as millions of South East Asians. It appeared that nobody wanted to think about it at all.

The war came to an end as it had begun; silently, unremarkably, very few Americans gave a damn.

It don't mean nothin'. {END}

www.ingramcontent.com/pod-product-compliance
Lightning Source LLC
Chambersburg PA
CBHW051218120626
46547CB00013B/1412